LEARNING TO WORSHIP WITH ALL YOUR HEART

A Study in the Biblical Foundations of Worship

Robert E. Webber

The Alleluia! Series of the Institute for Worship Studies

HENDRICKSON
PUBLISHERS

Hendrickson Publishers, Inc.
P. O. Box 3473
Peabody, Massachusetts 01961-3473

LEARNING TO WORSHIP WITH ALL YOUR HEART:
A Study in the Biblical Foundations of Worship
by Robert E. Webber

ISBN 1-56563-250-8

CONTENTS

WELCOME TO THE ALLELUIA! SERIES

This Bible study series has been designed by the Institute for Worship Studies primarily for laypersons in the church.

We are living in a time when worship has become a distinct priority for the church. For years, the church has emphasized evangelism, teaching, fellowship, missions, and service to society to the neglect of the very source of its power—worship. But in recent years we have witnessed a Spirit-led renewed interest in and practice of worship.

Because worship has been neglected for so many years, there is precious little information and teaching on the subject in our seminaries, Bible schools, and local churches.

The mission of The Institute for Worship Studies is to make the study of worship available to everyone in the church—academician, pastor, worship leader, music minister, and layperson.

Laypersons will find the seven courses of the Alleluia! series to be inspiring, informative, and life changing. Each course of study is rooted in biblical teaching, draws from the rich historical treasures of the church, and is highly practical and accessible.

The Institute for Worship Studies presents this course, *Learning to Worship with All Your Heart*, as a service to the local church and to its ministry of worship to God. May this study warm your heart, inform your mind, and kindle your spirit. May it inspire and set on fire the worship of the local church. And may this study minister to the church and to the One, Holy, Triune God in whose name it is offered.

THE SEVEN COURSES IN THE ALLELUIA! WORSHIP SERIES

Learning to Worship with All Your Heart—A Study in the Biblical Foundations of Worship.

You are led into the rich teachings of worship in both the Old and the New Testaments. Learn the vocabulary of worship, be introduced to theological themes, and study various descriptions of worship. Each lesson inspires you to worship at a deeper level—from the inside out.

Rediscovering the Missing Jewel—A Study of Worship through the Centuries.
This stretching course introduces you to the actual worship styles of Christians in other centuries and geographical locations. Study the history of the early, medieval, Reformation, modern, and contemporary periods of worship. Learn from them how your worship today may be enriched, inspired, and renewed. Each lesson introduces you to rich treasures of worship adaptable for contemporary use.

Renew Your Worship!—A Study in the Blending of Traditional and Contemporary Worship.
This inspiring course leads you into a deeper understanding and experience of your Sunday worship. How does worship bring the congregation into the presence of God, mold the people by the Word, and feed the believers spiritually? The answer to these and other questions will bring a new spiritual depth to our experience of worship.

Enter His Courts with Praise—A Study of the Role of Music and the Arts in Worship.
This course introduces you to the powerful way the arts can communicate the mystery of God at work in worship. Music, visual arts, drama, dance, and mime are seen as means through which the gospel challenges the congregation and changes lives.

Rediscovering the Christian Feasts—A Study in the Services of the Christian Year.
This stimulating and stretching course helps you experience the traditional church calendar with new eyes. It challenges the secular concept of time and shows how the practice of the Christian year offers an alternative to secularism and shapes the Christian's day-to-day experience of time, using the gospel as its grid.

Encountering the Healing Power of God—A Study in the Sacred Actions of Worship.
This course makes a powerful plea for the recovery of those sacred actions that shape the spiritual life. Baptism, Communion, anointing with oil, and other sacred actions are all interpreted with reflection on the death and resurrection of Jesus. These actions shape the believer's spiritual experience into a continual pattern of death to sin and rising to life in the Spirit.

Empowered by the Holy Spirit—A Study in the Ministries of Worship.
This course will challenge you to see the relationship between worship and life in the secular world. It empowers the believer in evangelism, spiritual formation, social action, care ministries, and other acts of love and charity.

Take all seven courses and earn a Certificate of Worship Studies (CWS). For more information, call the Institute for Worship Studies at (630) 510-8905

INTRODUCTION

Learning to Worship with All Your Heart: A Study in the Biblical Foundations of Worship may be used for personal study or a small-group course of study and spiritual formation. It is designed around thirteen easy-to-understand sessions. Each session has a two-part study guide. The first part is an individual study that each person completes privately. The second part is a one-hour interaction and application session that group members complete together (during the week or in an adult Sunday school setting). The first part helps you recall and reflect on what you've read, while the small-group study applies the material to each member's personal life and experience of public worship.

Learning to Worship with All Your Heart is designed for use by one or more people. When the course is used in a group setting, the person who is designated as the leader simply needs to lead the group through the lesson step by step. It is always best to choose a leader before you begin.

Here are some suggestions for making your group discussions lively and insightful.

SUGGESTIONS FOR THE STUDENT

A few simple guidelines will help you use the study guide most effectively. They can be summarized under three headings: Prepare, Participate, and Apply.

Prepare

1. Answer each question in the study guide, "Part I: Personal Study," thoughtfully and critically.

2. Do all your work prayerfully. Prayer itself is worship. As you increase your knowledge of worship, do so in a spirit of prayerful openness before God.

Participate

1. Don't be afraid to ask questions. Your questions may give voice to the other members in the group. Your courage in speaking out will give others permission to talk and may encourage more stimulating discussion.

2. Don't hesitate to share your personal experiences. Abstract thinking has its place, but personal illustrations will help you and others remember the material more vividly.

3. Be open to others. Listen to the stories that other members tell, and respond to them in a way that does not invalidate their experiences.

Apply

1. Always ask yourself, "How can this apply to worship?"

2. Commit yourself to being a more intentional worshiper. Involve yourself in what is happening around you.

3. Determine your gifts. Ask yourself, "What can I do in worship that will minister to the body of Christ?" Then offer your gifts and talents to worship.

SUGGESTIONS FOR THE LEADER

Like the worship that it advocates, the group study in *Learning to Worship with All Your Heart* is dialogic in nature. Because this study has been developed around the principles of discussion and sharing, a monologue or lecture approach will not work. The following guidelines will help you encourage discussion, facilitate learning, and implement the practice of worship. Use these guidelines with "Part II: Group Discussion" in each session.

1. Encourage the participants to prepare thoroughly and to bring their Bibles and study guides to each session.

2. Begin each session with prayer. Since worship is a kind of prayer, learning about worship should be a prayerful experience.

3. Discuss each question individually. Ask for several answers and encourage people to react to comments made by others.

4. Use a chalkboard or flip chart or dry-erase board. Draw charts and symbols that visually enhance the ideas being presented. Outline major concepts.

5. Look for practical applications of answers and suggestions that are offered. Try asking questions like, "How would you include this in our worship?" "How would you feel about that change?" "How does this insight help you to be a better worshiper?"

6. Invite concrete personal illustrations. Ask questions like, "Have you experienced that? Where? When? Describe how you felt in that particular situation."

7. When you have concluded Session 13, send the names and addresses of all the students who will complete the class to: Institute for Worship Studies, Box 894, Wheaton, IL 60189. We will then send a certificate of accomplishment for each student in time for you to distribute them during the last class. The cost of each certificate is $1.00. (Add $3.00 for postage and handling.)

One final suggestion: Purchase the larger work upon which this course is based, volume 1 of *The Complete Library of Christian Worship*. This volume, entitled *The Biblical Foundations of Christian Worship*, comprises a beautiful 8½-by-11-inch coffee table book that will inform your mind and inspire your heart through hours of reading and study.

PART I

WORSHIP AND THE STORY OF SALVATION

CELEBRATE!

A Study in the Event That Worship Celebrates

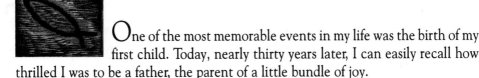 One of the most memorable events in my life was the birth of my first child. Today, nearly thirty years later, I can easily recall how thrilled I was to be a father, the parent of a little bundle of joy.

When we brought that miniature human being home, one of my first outings with him was to take him to the seminary where I taught so I could show him off. I walked across the campus, holding him in my arms, and stopped everyone I met and said proudly, "Meet my son, John."

And when John turned one and ten and twenty, and we gathered to celebrate his birth, I'd say, "Hey, John. I've got this story to tell you." Then I'd tell and act out how I walked across the campus, joyfully displaying him and saying, "Meet my son, John."

I tell you this story because I want you to think about the important events of your life that you celebrate with words, actions, and festivity. But more important, I want you to see the connection between celebrating these important life-events and celebrating the events of history in which God was at work, bringing salvation to you and to the world.

Worship is about celebrating events. Worship celebrates God's saving acts in history. Let's study this idea.

GOD TAKES THE INITIATIVE

I'll begin by telling you about a prayer I heard while visiting a church. The prayer captures the biblical notion that God initiates a relationship with us, a relationship we celebrate in worship.

After leading the congregation in singing a hymn, the worship leader said, "Let us pray," and he spoke this prayer: "Lord, we bless You for creating us in Your image. And we thank You that after we fell away from You into sin You did not leave us in our sin, but You came to us in Jesus Christ, who lived, died, and was resurrected for our salvation. Now, as we await His coming again, receive our worship in His name. Amen."

When I heard this prayer, I wanted to shout or jump for joy. Here was the whole story of salvation from creation to re-creation, summarized in a few sentences. And the emphasis was not primarily on me or even on my experience, but on God, who initiates a saving action toward a creation and creatures in desperate need of healing and salvation. The history of the Bible is how God continually initiates a relationship with us. In this study we look at how God initiated a relationship with Abraham, with Israel, and now with us through Jesus Christ. This story is recalled in worship, and it is to this message that we respond to in our worship.

God Initiates a Relationship with Abraham

Have you ever done anything that required an unusual risk? Abraham was living a comfortable existence in Ur of the Chaldees when God said, "I want you to pack your bags and go on an unknown journey" (see Heb. 11:8). "I'll go before you," said God, "but right now I choose not to tell you all the details. But I will tell you this: If you obey Me I will bless you greatly. I will make a great nation of you and I will bless the whole world through you." Abraham did just what God asked him to do. Here is what lies at the heart of salvation and of worship: God initiates a relationship, and we respond.

God Initiates a Relationship with Israel

The next great saving deed of God in history occurred when God delivered the people of Israel from captivity to Pharaoh and led them across the Red Sea, to enter into covenant with them at Mount Sinai.

The prayer that worship leader prayed was right. God does not leave us in captivity or in bondage to the enemy. God liberates us, freeing us from those powers of evil that would enslave and destroy our lives. The Exodus event is a resounding testimony to this fundamental truth of biblical faith.

The book of Exodus tells of Israel's plight. But more important it tells the story of God's redeeming power, a story that the people of Israel retell in the Passover seder every year.

Ask a Jew, "What is the most important event in Jewish history?" The answer you will likely get is "the Exodus event." Why? Because in that event God delivered the people from the power of Pharaoh and became their God, and they became the people of God.

Today, more than four thousand years later, Jews all over the world remember, recall, and enact that event in Passover celebration.

GOD INITIATES A RELATIONSHIP WITH US THROUGH JESUS CHRIST

Christians have always seen the Exodus event as a type of the great New Testament event of the death and resurrection of Jesus.

All people are in bondage to evil, to the powers and principalities, to the sins of the flesh.

But the story continues.

God does not leave us in our sin. God comes to us in Jesus Christ. "God," proclaims the New Testament, "was reconciling the world to himself in Christ" (2 Cor. 5:19). God, in Jesus Christ, binds the powers of evil (Matt. 12:22–29), dethrones the powers of evil (Col. 2:15), and will ultimately destroy the powers of evil (Rev. 20–22).

So now, when we gather together for worship, like Israel in the Passover, we tell and reenact the old, old story of Jesus and His love. A passage that captures the essence of biblical worship is given to us by Peter, who says that we have been called to proclaim the wonderful deeds of God, who brought us out of darkness into marvelous light. (1 Pet. 2:9)

WHAT DOES IT MEAN TO CELEBRATE?

Now that we have established the idea that worship celebrates God's saving deeds in history, we need to look at the word *celebrate*.

I love a celebration. I think the whole world loves to celebrate. But to truly celebrate, there needs to be something for us to celebrate. Have you ever tried to celebrate for the sake of celebration? I have, and it always seems empty!

A true celebration is characterized by three things:

1. It is rooted in an event.
2. It makes the event become contemporaneous with the group celebrating.
3. It is full of stories, singing, feasting, dramatizing, and enacting.

Let me give you an example. I told you earlier that during my oldest child's birthday parties, I would tell and act out the story of bringing him home from the hospital. In that reenactment, three things were happening. First, I was telling about a real event. Second, the power and significance of that event were made real to the people gathered to celebrate his birth—that is, it was made contemporaneous. And third, we celebrated his birth by telling stories, by festooning with balloons, cakes, drama, and the like.

Now let's see how this relates to worship.

When we gather to worship together we are celebrating the most important events in human history—the events through which God brings salvation to the world. Through our celebration, these events become contemporaneous to us. That is, the saving and healing power of God become available to the worshiping community. How do we do it? We tell the story; we dramatize it, sing it, and festoon it. In this way we celebrate God's saving deeds. This is exactly the way the people of Israel celebrated their liberation from Pharaoh. So the church, continuing the practice of the Israelites' worship, celebrates the saving deed of God in Jesus through proclaiming, reenacting, singing, and responding to the death and resurrection of Jesus Christ, which accomplished our salvation and set the pattern of our living.

CONCLUSION

This study now brings us to the place where we can attempt a definition of public worship. Worship is not easy to define because it is so rich and deep. But central to worship is what follows: In worship the church gathers to celebrate God's saving deeds. Through this celebration, God continually brings to the worshiper the benefit of His saving deeds—the forgiveness of sin and the healing of life, which flows from the saving and healing death and resurrection of Jesus Christ.

STUDY GUIDE

Read Session 1, "Celebrate!,"
before answering these questions.

PART I: PERSONAL STUDY

Complete the following questions individually.

1. Life Connection

◆ In Session 1 we have talked about the importance of events. Identify an important spiritual event in your life. Do you enjoy remembering this event? Do you tell others the story of this event? Summarize the event here. My recommittment of my life to Christ @ Jesus 76. I remember praying @ Brian Rudd. I do tell people about that event. He preached on being eagles and we stomped on Satan!

2. Content Questions

◆ Drawing from the text, make a time line of God's saving deeds in biblical history. (Go beyond the text, including as many saving events and people in the line of God's saving action that come to mind.)

◆ How does the Jewish Passover help us to understand Christian worship?

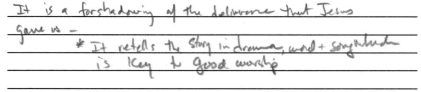

It is a forshadowing of the deliverance that Jesus gave us —
   * It retells the story in drama, word + song which is key to good worship

- How does worship remember? _It looks at saving history in Scripture in retelling the story_

enact? _It uses symbols & drama, Sacramental actions_

celebrate? _It leads people to rejoice - singing, Praising_

3. *Scripture Study*

- Read Exodus 12:1–14. What are the Israelites to commemorate (v. 14)?
  The Lord's Passing over Them and not visiting them with death because the lamb's blood was applied to the Door frames of Their house

- Read 1 Peter 2:9–10. How does this passage affirm worship as the celebration of the Christ-event? _It stresses The "before" God state we were in and The "now in Him" state we have. - We are all priests of God — called to worship - so That we may declare His Praise. out of darkness - into light; Also with Mercy -_

- Read Deuteronomy 6:20–25. How does the story get told in worship?
  It is made contemporary - "we" includes the generations that followed the one experiencing the initial event. - Promises of God continue & belong to the following generations. There is a tie between commands + decrees and God's actions

4. *Application*

- Think about a recent worship service in your church. How were the events of the living, dying, and rising of Christ expressed in Scripture, sermon, song, and prayer during this service? (You may want to look at a recent bulletin to refresh your memory.) *Communion Remarks Christs life.*
Songs told after resurrection. Scripture focused on Emmaus Road.

PART II: GROUP DISCUSSION

The following questions are designed for group discussion. Share the insights you gained from your personal study in Part I.

Write out all answers that group members give to the questions on a chalkboard, a flip chart, or a dry erase board.

1. *Life Connection*

- Begin by having several members of the group share an event that they love to remember.

2. *Thought Questions*

- Compare the time lines each member of the group made to visualize God's saving events in history. Does God continue to work today?

- Compare the experiences the members of this group may have had with a Jewish Passover or with a Christian version of the Passover. How does this experience remember, reenact, and celebrate God's work of salvation for Israel?

- Do you think Christian worship contains stories and symbols akin to those of the Hebrew Passover?

- Share insights into how Christian worship asks us to remember, reenact, and celebrate.

3. *Scripture Study*

- What do the Israelites commemorate in worship? (See Exod. 12:1–14.)

- Does 1 Peter 2:9–10 affirm Christian worship as a commemoration of God's saving action in Christ? Explain your answer.

- Is it appropriate for us to read Deuteronomy 5:20–25 as a mandate for Christians as well as for Jews to hand down God's saving deeds through the story of worship?

4. *Application*

- How does the content of the worship of your local church need to change in order to be a celebration of the substance of worship, the re-membering and reenacting of God's work of salvation? (Think in terms of Scripture, sermon, prayers, hymns and songs, Communion, the Christian year, sacraments, and ordinances.)

- How does your church's style of worship need to change in order for your worship to be a celebration of God's work of salvation?

- How has this lesson helped you to better understand worship as a celebration?

THE POWER OF MEMORY

A Study in the Recollection of God's Saving Deeds

I'm not one of those persons who hates to admit that he's getting older. The fact of life is that I've passed through six decades. Frankly, it has happened so fast that, like others, I say, "I don't know where the time went."

As I've gotten older I've become more and more sensitive to memory. Of course, all of us have memories we would like to forget. That's natural and part of life. But all of us also have memories that we savor—memories that bring back good feelings and good times. The older I get, the more I enjoy savoring the good memories. I'm sure you have many good memories that you like to recall, too.

WORSHIP REMEMBERS THE SALVATION STORY

If you have ever worshiped in a synagogue or gone to a Passover seder or celebrated a Jewish holiday, then you are aware that Jewish worship is rooted in memory.

The primary memory is that God brought the people of Israel out of Egypt, formed them into a community, entered into covenant with them, gave them the Torah, and promised to bring them into the promised land.

The Exodus was the event upon which Israel was founded. This event was central, determinative, and necessary to what Israel was all about as God's people. Therefore, worship is a continual reminder of that event. When Israel became indifferent to or forgot the Exodus, Israel went into spiritual and moral decline. But when Israel remembered the event and allowed it to shape the nation's life once again, Israel was blessed by God.

Christian worship follows the same pattern. It remembers the event that is central, determinative, and necessary to what the church is as the people of God: Christ's crucifixion and resurrection.

WORSHIP AS HISTORICAL RECITATION

I not only savor good memories, but I like to talk about them too. I'll tell anyone who will listen about my childhood in Africa, about my trip to Russia, or about the special experiences I've had with God and with God's people.

Biblical worship is like that. It likes to remember the stories of God's saving deeds.

In the Bible we find summaries of God's saving action. For example, there's a great story of how God redeemed Israel in Deuteronomy 26:5–9. And in the New Testament, Timothy provides us with a marvelous summary of God's action in Christ (1 Tim. 3:16).

Biblical hymns were also written so that God's people could remember God's saving deeds. Look, for example, at Miriam's song in Exodus 15 and think about how this great story recounts, recalls, and rejoices in the deliverance of Israel from the hands of Pharaoh.

And then there is the striking hymn, sung in Philippians, about how God humbled Himself and became one of us, and how in the end of history every knee shall bow and every tongue confess that Jesus Christ is Lord (Phil. 2:6–11).

These stories are the memories of the Christian faith, the very stuff of worship!

WORSHIP AS DRAMATIC REPRESENTATION

Usually, when I tell someone a story, I act it out. I talk with my hands and face, and sometimes I'll even jump up and act out my story with my full body. You probably do the same thing.

This idea of acting out what we say—or somehow physically presenting the story we tell—lies at the very heart of worship.

Biblical worship is not just story; it is drama. At the Passover, Israel dramatizes its redemption from Egypt, and it does so with great attention to detail, paying great attention to dress, food, movement, and gesture.

But what Jews do, Christians do as well. When we gather at the Lord's Table to remember Christ's death and resurrection, we do drama. We not only say the words, but we also add actions to the words. We gather around the table, we break the bread, we lift the cup, we eat, and we drink. And in all these movements we make remembrance.

CONCLUSION

Memory is very important to all of us—to our own individual lives, to our families, to our churches, to our nation. As we recall the important events that shape our lives, we are often filled with joy. Biblical worship is just like that. It recalls, remembers, and enacts God's saving deeds. And in that action there is much joy.

STUDY GUIDE

Read Session 2, "The Power of Memory,"
before starting the study guide

PART 1: PERSONAL STORY

Complete the following questions individually.

1. Life Connection

+ In this lesson we have been reminded of the importance of memory. Identify a spiritual event or experience from your past that is important to
  you. It may be your conversion, your baptism, a special retreat or worship. Jot down your memory here: *Jesus '76 and praying with*
  Brian Rudd — I remember him talking about eagles nests
  and God getting us to fly and that we could defeat
  Satan — and jumping up and down on "the devil"

2. Content Questions

+ How does the Jewish Passover remember the Exodus event? _____
  Retells the story — they eat matya and roasted meat and
  recline — They eat bitter herbs and salt water for tears.

+ How does Christian worship remember the event of the life, death, and
  resurrection of Christ? *@ communion — Break the bread*
  for Christ's body and pour juice for Christ's blood.

+ Think of a song you know that remembers the Christ-event and write it
  here: *O sacred Head now wounded — with grief and grief bowed down ·*
  Mine, mine was the transgression — Mine the thorny crown .

+ Think of a drama you know that remembers the Christ-event and write
  its title here: _____ *Ben Hur*

STUDY GUIDE

3. *Scripture Study*

◆ Read Deuteronomy 26:5–9. Make a time line here of the events remembered in this creed.

Jacob to goes Egypt — Became a great nation — Jews mistreated — Cry to The Lord 400 years — The Lord brought us out of Egypt — Enter the promise land.

◆ Read Exodus 15:1–21. Find in this song at least three things Israel remembered from Yahweh's saving action for them. Write them here.

1. The horse + rider (Pharaoh's army) thrown into the sea.
2. Divided the Red Sea
3. Lead the people in the wilderness.

◆ Read Philippians 2:6–11. Summarize in your own words what this song remembers.

1. Jesus was God in Heaven
2. Jesus became human Servant
3. Obedient to death on a cross.
4. God exalted Him above all others
5. One day all people will acknowledge Him

4. *Application*

◆ Get ready for the group discussions by jotting below how the power of memory is at work in the worship of your church. Do you find it in songs, prayers, Scripture, sermons, baptisms, Communion? How may memory in the worship of your church be made more clear? We could state more clearly "why" we do what we do. We could talk about songs more before we sing them.

PART II: GROUP DISCUSSION

The following questions draw on the study of Part I. Share the insights gained in your personal study and learn from each other.

Write on a chalkboard or flip chart all of the group members' answers to the questions in each section.

1. Life Connection

◆ Begin by having several members of the group share the memory of a special spiritual event. Comment primarily on the experience of memory.

2. Thought Questions

◆ How important is memory to our spiritual health? Does a memory of a spiritual event or experience in our lives remind us of who we are and to whom we belong? (Inquire in depth about this question and probe its significance in the life of each member of the group.)

3. Scripture Study

◆ What do we remember in worship? How does memory define us as a people?

◆ Read Deuteronomy 26:5–9. Share the time lines students made of this passage. How many events are remembered in this brief statement?

◆ Below is the Apostles' Creed, ecumenical version. Read it together. On the chalkboard or flip chart, list the events this creed remembers.

> I believe in God the Father Almighty,
>   creator of heaven and earth.
>
> I believe in Jesus Christ, his only Son, our Lord,
>   who was conceived by the Holy Spirit,
>   born of the Virgin Mary,
>   suffered under Pontius Pilate,
>   was crucified, died, and was buried;
>   he descended to the dead.
>   On the third day he rose again;
>   he ascended into heaven,
>   is seated at the right hand of the Father,
>   and will come again to judge the living and the dead.

> I believe in the Holy Spirit,
>   the holy catholic church,
>   the communion of saints,
>   the forgiveness of sins,
>   the resurrection of the body
>   and the life everlasting. Amen.

◆ Read Exodus 14:1–31. Have each group member share his or her insights into this song. How many aspects of God's saving deeds are found here? List them together.

   Next, in a hymnal or other songbook, find one or two songs that express a memory of God's saving deeds. How many "memory" hymns can the group find?

◆ Read Philippians 2:6–11. Share each other's insights into this song. What does it remember? Write it on the board.

   Identify a hymn or song that expresses the theme of this Scripture passage. Ask group members how they feel when they sing this song.

4. Application

◆ Evaluate your worship experience and find ways to incorporate memory more effectively in your worship. You may need to refer to a bulletin or order from a recent service.

◆ Think through a recent service and identify as many words, songs, acts, and symbols as you can that are reminders of God's saving actions.

◆ What needs to be added to your worship to bring to mind God's saving actions?

◆ Should worship remind you of God's saving actions not only in biblical history, but also in your life? How could this be accomplished?

◆ How did this lesson improve your understanding of worship?

◆ How did this lesson improve your ability to worship?

REHEARSING OUR RELATIONSHIP WITH GOD

A Study in the Place of Covenant in Worship

My wife has a saying that I really like and wish I could claim to have created. She says, "Keeping agreements is what makes life work." I make all kinds of agreements—agreements with my spouse, my children, my friends; agreements to perform my duties as a teacher; agreements with my publishers to meet deadlines; and many more agreements—and I keep them. They are important to me, central to my responsibilities, and crucial in all my relationships.

Take some time to think about your agreements in marriage, the family, and work. Having done this, you will be able to make a connection with a vital aspect of worship: the place of the covenant in worship, or what we call in popular language, agreements.

GOD'S AGREEMENT WITH ISRAEL

What lies at the heart of God's relationship with Israel is a covenant—an agreement made between God and Israel. We frequently find this covenant expressed in short form here and there in Scripture: "I will be their God and they shall be my people" (see Gen. 17:7; Lev. 26:12, 45; Deut. 29:10–13).

Essentially, God said to Israel, "I'll be your God. I'll give you my name. I'll bless you, and I'll give you the promised land. What I want from you is undivided loyalty and complete obedience. I also want your love, and I want your worship. And I also want you to love each other."

Israel agreed. So the covenant between God and Israel was ratified in a public act of worship. The people of Israel agreed to keep "the book of the covenant," and the relationship between God and Israel was sealed in a sacrifice and blood ritual. Israel's entire history and all of its worship life were tied into this agreement.

Unfortunately, Israel was not that good at keeping the agreement. But God was faithful to the covenant.

GOD'S COVENANT WITH THE CHURCH

Just as God entered into covenant with Israel, so also God entered into covenant with the church.

While the covenant stipulations with the church are similar to those God made with Israel—I will be your God and you will be my people—there is a difference.

That difference is Jesus Christ. Israel wasn't able to keep the covenant. The people fell away from their agreements again and again.

But in this new covenant, Jesus Christ does for Israel and for the church—for us and for everyone—what we cannot do for ourselves. He keeps the agreement. He fulfills the covenant. And in His absolute obedience He establishes for us an eternal relationship with God. Nowhere is this truth more clearly expressed than in the book of Hebrews (see chaps. 9–10).

THE COVENANTS COMPARED

Worship in the Old Testament, just like worship in the New Testament, is based on the agreement between God and God's people.

Israel first had access to Jehovah through Moses, who entered the presence of God, spoke with God face to face, and interceded on behalf of the nation.

Then God instituted the sacrificial system of the tabernacle and later the temple as the way to approach Him. (This will be studied in Session 4.)

Now we approach God in the name of Jesus Christ—our elder brother who has kept covenant with the Father for us. Our calling is to keep the agreement we have made with God: to love God with our whole heart; to be obedient to all God expects of us; to love all people and to gather again and again to remember our agreement (and the story of our relationship to God); and to continually live by that agreement.

CONCLUSION

In this study of the covenant, we gain another insight into worship and how through worship our relationship to God is maintained, repaired, and transformed.

Think about your own acts of public worship and ask yourself: "What happens in my worship that reflects the agreements I have made with God?"

One more thing to think about: Does this worship fill you with joy?

STUDY GUIDE

Read Session 3, "Rehearsing Our Relationship with God,"
before starting the study guide.

PART I: PERSONAL STORY

Complete the following questions individually.

1. *Life Connection*

♦ Take some time to think about all the agreements you have made. Is it true for you that "keeping agreements is what makes life work"? Choose one agreement that you have made and jot down below how that agreement defines and organizes your life. It is true that keeping agreements is what makes life work. I made an agreement with Susan to love her and be faithful to her. Under that agreement, we have 3 daughters, we care for each other and we help each other through life in supporting each other.

2. *Content Questions*

♦ What is the agreement God made with Israel? He would be their God, Give them His name, bless them and give them the promised land. They were to give undivided loyalty and complete obedience. They were to love Him, worship Him and love each other.

♦ What is the agreement God made with the church? Jesus does for us what we could not do for ourselves. Jesus fulfills the covenant. - We are called to love God, worship Him, love others & remember to covenant & live by it.

♦ What is the difference between the covenant made with Israel and that made with the church? _The covenant @ Israel was marked by ceremonial actions and stipulation and rules which the Israelites couldn't keep. With the church - Jesus has kept the covenant stipulations on our behalf._

3. *Scripture Study*

♦ Read Deuteronomy 6:1–8. What is the commandment Israel agrees to keep? Write it here: _Love the Lord your God with all your heart, and with all your soul and with all your strength. These commandments to be upon your hearts. Impress Them on your children all the time. Tie them as symbals on your hands; bind them on your foreheads._

♦ Write down the many ways God gave Israel to remember the agreement. _Talk about Them Tie them on their foreheads and arms Put Them on their door frames._

♦ What are the results of Israel's keeping the agreement. _Blessing. Fear of the Lord, Enjoy long life. Things may go well, you may increase greatly._

♦ Read Exodus 24:1–8. Is this a worship setting? _Outdoor altar worship. It is worship because they are remembering the covenant and ratifying it as a group._

♦ What agreement do God and Israel make in this worship setting? _They are agree to live by the covenant._

- What action seals this agreement? Write it here: _____

  1. Verbal agreement of the people - vs 3

  2. Verbal   "   "   " - vs 7

  3. Sealing People @ blood vs. 8

- Read Hebrews 8:1–13. Why did God find fault with the old covenant?

  The people didn't keep it. It was external to them

- What are the distinguishing features of the new covenant? _____

  The law will be in their minds + hearts. They will be taught
  by God - each will know O. - God will forgive their
  wickedness and not remember their sin any more

4. *Application*

   Get ready for the group discussion by thinking through the agreements recited and rehearsed in worship.

- Does worship rehearse the agreement God has made with us? _yes_

- When and where in your worship does the rehearsal of God's covenant (agreement) find expression? (Think about the content of hymns, creeds, Scripture, sermons, Communion, baptism.) _Prayers , Creeds,_
  Scripture

- How may the worship of your congregation incorporate the agreement between God and His people more effectively? _Regularly - recite._
  Creed as a remembrance of the Covenant

PART II: GROUP DISCUSSION

The following questions draw on the study of Part I. Share the insights gained in your personal study and learn from each other.

Write on a chalkboard or flip chart all of the group members' answers to the questions in each section.

1. *Life Connection*
- Begin by having several members of the group share the agreement that defines and organizes their lives. Ask each member how important agreements are to his or her life.

2. *Thought Questions*
- Find in Scripture several examples of agreements that were made but broken (start with Adam). List these agreements on the chalkboard or flip chart.
- What were the effects of these broken agreements? Write the answers on the chalkboard or flip chart.
- How do group members respond to the idea that worship is a rehearsal of the agreement God makes with us? Has anyone ever thought of this idea before? How does it inform your view of worship?

3. *Scripture Study*
- Read Deuteronomy 6:1–8. Does this passage say, "If you keep my commandments it will go well with you"? What does that mean? Spiritual health? Wealth? Power?
- The Ten Commandments were read in synagogue worship. Should we read the commandments in our worship?
- Read Exodus 24:1–8. How does the worship of Israel rehearse the agreement with God? Should Christian worship rehearse the agreement between God and God's people more clearly? How would you do this?
- Read Hebrew's 8:1–13. Ask several people to explain in their own words what this text is saying. How does the truth of this text affect the way we worship?

4. *Application*

- The thrust of this study is to show how worship is a rehearsal of the agreement made between God and God's people. In worship, one may say, we rehearse our relationship to God.

- How does the notion that worship is a rehearsal of our relationship to God affect the way you think about worship?

- Identify and list aspects of worship in your local church that do, in fact, rehearse your relationship to God.

- What needs to happen in your local church to make worship a rehearsal of relationship with God more clear?

- How will Session 3 help you to experience the meaning of worship more fully?

- Evaluate your worship experience and find ways to incorporate memory more effectively in your worship. You may need to refer to a bulletin or order from a recent service.

- Think through a recent service and identify as many words, songs, acts, and symbols as you can that are reminders of God's saving actions.

- What needs to be added to your worship to bring to mind God's saving actions?

- Should worship remind you of God's saving actions not only in biblical history, but also in your life? How could this be accomplished?

- How did this lesson improve your understanding of worship?

- How did this lesson improve your ability to worship?

An Offering of Praise

A Study in the Concept of Sacrifice in Worship

Most of us who live in the United States and in the wealthier countries of the world know little about sacrifice. We don't live in a culture that practices ritual sacrifices in either civil acts or in acts of worship. So where do we go to make connection with the concept of sacrifice in biblical faith?

This assignment is not an easy one. All of us know about ritual sacrifice through our exposure to other civilizations, and we have more than likely heard of cultic sacrifices that are being conducted in satanic worship. But we really don't live in an age of sacrifice, so the ritual meaning of the term is not familiar to us, even if we know about the concept.

Sacrifice in the Old Testament

In the Old Testament, covenants between God and people are always secured through the ritual enactment of a sacrifice. Some examples of people with whom God made covenants are Noah (Gen. 3:20–9:17); Abram (Gen. 15:1–21); Isaac (Gen. 26:24–25); Jacob (Gen. 31:43–55; 35:6–12); and Moses on behalf of Israel (Exod. 24:1–8).

Today when we make agreements with each other we don't make a sacrifice, but we do make signs and acts to express that agreement.

For example, my daughter recently got married. While I attend weddings on a fairly regular basis, I don't always pay careful attention to every detail. But this time, since it was my own flesh and blood, I watched and listened more intently. What I rediscovered was the many sign-acts that the marrying couple go through. Showers and parties, rehearsal, walking down the aisle, exchanging vows and rings, lighting the unity candle, the kiss, the reception, throwing the bouquet, rice throwing, and more after-the-wedding rituals are all part of a highly symbolic language that speaks joyfully of a new beginning in marriage.

So it is in worship. Worship is full of sign-acts that speak the language of relationship.

God gave Israel a sacrificial system that was full of sign-acts, signifying their approach to God in worship. A fundamental sign of relationship with God was expressed in the sacrifices at the tabernacle and in the very setting of time, space, and ritual on which these sacrifices were accomplished. It was in this sign-act space that Israel conducted the sacrifices that were part of the covenant and expressed the relationship between God and Israel.

Many of the sacrifices Israel conducted were for the sake of atonement. The meaning of the word *atonement* has been caught in popular language by a play on the word—at one with God.

A vital part of the story of worship for both Israel and Christians is the need to acknowledge and to deal with sin.

In the Old Testament, the people of Israel dealt with sin through the sacrifice of animals. The most important of all the sacrifices for sin was celebrated on the Day of Atonement.

In the New Testament, Jesus is the once-for-all sacrifice for sin.

SACRIFICE IN THE NEW TESTAMENT

Sacrifice is central to New Testament worship. But things are different now. We no longer need to make bloody sacrifices, because the once-for-all sacrifice of Jesus Christ made all other sacrifices unnecessary.

In worship we proclaim the sacrifice of Christ through Scripture readings, sermons, hymns, prayers, and especially at the Lord's Table. At the Lord's Table we offer what is called the prayer of thanksgiving, which ranges from an extemporaneous prayer given by an elder or deacon to the written prayers of the liturgical church. The important part of this ritual eating of bread and drinking of wine is that the church remembers and gives thanks. We do not repeat the once-for-all sacrifice of Christ on the cross, but we do remember the sacrifice and covenant God made with us, ratified by the death of Christ. Because Christ is our sacrifice, we are free from having to make any sacrifice as God's people did in the Old Testament. Instead, through the bread and wine of Communion, we offer God our sacrifices of praise and thanksgiving. This is why the early church and contemporary liturgical churches call Communion the Eucharist (which means "to make thanks").

CONCLUSION

Think about the whole subject of sacrifice, because it opens up an aspect of thought that is vital to our worship. Christians worship through that once-for-all sacrifice of Jesus Christ. What we bring to worship is not an animal sacrifice, as in the Old Testament, but we come to worship in the name of Jesus and we bring the sacrifice of praise and thanksgiving. In this way we worship, glorify, and honor God's holy name.

STUDY GUIDE

Read Session 4, "An Offering of Praise,"
before starting the study guide.

PART I: PERSONAL STUDY

Complete the following questions individually.

1. *Life Connection*

◆ Because you are not from a culture that uses sacrificial rites, it will be more difficult for you to make a life connection with this lesson. If you have had experience of another culture that does sacrifice or if you know of another person who has, then write that experience below. If not, then think in terms of a sign-act (a ring or something that expresses a re-lationship) and write about that below, commenting on why this sign-act has meaning for you. _____

_____

_____

_____

_____

2. *Content Questions*

◆ What does the sacrificial system of Old Testament worship signify?

_____

_____

_____

◆ Did many of the Old Testament sacrifices deal with the matter of sin?

_____

_____

◆ What did these sacrifices accomplish? _____

_____

_____

_____

◆ What is the sacrifice in the New Testament? _____

_____

_____

_____

◆ What is the sacrifice God wants from us? _____

_____

_____

_____

◆ What sacrifice do we bring in worship? _____

_____

_____

_____

3. *Scripture Study*

◆ Read Genesis 8:20–22. Why did Noah build an altar to God? Was it a response of praise and thanksgiving? _____

_____

_____

_____

◆ What was God's response to Noah's sacrifice? _____

_____

_____

_____

◆ Read Exodus 24:1–8. Why was this sacrifice offered to God?

_____

_____

_____

◆ What is the agreement expressed in this sacrifice? _____

_____

_____

_____

◆ Read Hebrews 9:28. Why is the sacrifice Christ made greater than the Old Testament sacrifices? _____

_____

_____

_____

◆ Read 1 Corinthians 11:23–26. What does the Lord's Supper proclaim?

_____

_____

_____

_____

◆ In the same sentence, Paul says that the Lord's death is proclaimed

_____

_____

4. *Application*

Get ready for the group discussion by thinking about the relationship of sacrifice to worship. These questions will help you.

◆ When Communion is celebrated in your local church, what do you think the church is doing? _____

_____

_____

_____

_____

◆ Should Communion be a sober experience or a joyful one?

_____

_____

_____

♦ How often should Communion be celebrated? Why? _____

_____

_____

_____

_____

_____

PART II: GROUP DISCUSSION

The following questions are designed for group discussion. Share the insights you gained from your personal study in Part I.

Write out all answers that group members give to the questions on a chalkboard, a flip chart, or a dry erase board.

1. *Life Connection*
♦ Begin the group study by sharing the life connections several members of the group were able to make with the concept of sacrifice.

2. *Thought Questions*
♦ Why was sacrifice so important to worship in the Old Testament?
♦ Is it possible to worship God without a sacrifice?
♦ Why is there no longer a need for the sacrificial system of the Old Testament?
♦ If there is no need for sacrifice in Christianity, what, then, is the role of the Lord's Supper?
♦ Do you think the New Testament emphasis on the Lord's Supper is primarily a description of what the early Christians did or a prescription for us to follow?

3. *Scripture Study*
♦ Read Genesis 8:20–22. Why did Noah build an altar to God? Should we build some kind of physical or perhaps spiritual altar to God in our homes or in our hearts? Have members explain their answers.

- Read Exodus 24:1–8. Why do you think sacrifice was such an important part of Old Testament worship?
- Do you think sacrifice should be a more important part of your public worship? What would it look like?
- Read Hebrews 9:23–28. Summarize what the author is saying. What does this passage say about your worship?
- Read 1 Corinthians 11:23–26. Should the contemporary church celebrate the Lord's Supper more frequently? Why?

4. *Application*

The thrust of this study is to show that an agreement between God and God's people has from the very beginning been sealed with a sacrifice. We must ask how this idea applies to our weekly worship.

- What expressions of sacrifice are found in the worship of your congregation?
- What role does sacrifice play in Christian worship?
- What do you think it means to say that we, the people of the worshiping community, "bring the sacrifice of praise"?
- Should the church celebrate the Lord's Supper more frequently?

PART II

WORSHIP

AND THE

RESPONSE

OF GOD'S

PEOPLE

LET PRAISE BE ON OUR LIPS

A Study in the Old Testament Vocabulary of Worship

I like for people to thank me when I've done something for them or when I've done my job right. I'm not embarrassed to admit this, because I think we are all that way. Who wants to pour out an enormous amount of energy for someone or for a project and not be acknowledged? It is normal and healthy to expect to be acknowledged.

WORDS OF WORSHIP

Although I want to be thanked and sometimes at least praised, I don't want to be worshiped.

Things are a bit different with God. God wants to be thanked and praised, and God also wants to be worshiped. Worship is part of what God's covenant with us is all about. In the covenant, God says, "This is what I have done and will do for you." In worship we say thank you and praise God with all our heart.

But what is this work called worship? We have seen that it begins with God's initiative, that it remembers the story of God's saving deeds, that it rehearses our relation to God through the covenant, and that it demands the sacrifice of praise and obedience.

But now we can come to understand a little more about worship through certain definitions:

Worship means—
+ to bow down;
+ to give thanks;
+ to know that the Lord is God;
+ to trust in God's covenant;
+ to fear the Lord;
+ to seek the presence of the Lord;

- to wait upon the Lord;
- to intercede.

WORDS FOR EXPRESSIONS OF PRAISE AND ACCLAMATION

While the words we use in worship tell us what worship means, other words tell us how to "do the meaning." That is, insights into heart attitude tell us how to do what God wants. In worship, we are to:

- "boast" in God's deeds;
- make high and extol the Lord;
- ascribe greatness to God;
- raise a shout; and
- be joyful!

CONCLUSION

In this session, we see that God wants to be worshiped; God loves to be worshiped. In worship we tell God the truth about God—we praise God and offer God our thankful voices and hearts not only because of the story of salvation, but also because of the very character of the God who would seek us out to restore us to Himself.

Read Session 5, "Let Praise Be on Our Lips,"
before starting the study guide.

PART I: PERSONAL STUDY

Complete the following questions individually.

1. *Life Connection*

◆ Because worship has to do with remembering and giving thanks, in this
exercise you'll want to get in touch with those themes in your own life.
Take a few minutes to remember something you did for someone and
how you felt when that person responded by remembering and sending
you thanks. Now, think of a time you did something for someone who
did nor remember your kindness and did not return thanks. How did you
feel in each situation? Write your responses here: _____

_____

_____

_____

_____

2. *Content Questions*

◆ Study the words of worship below. Match each word or phrase to its definition.

____ An expression of confidence	a. bow down
____ An intellectual apprehension	b. give thanks
____ A physical action	c. know that the Lord is God
____ An emotional response	d. trust in God's covenant
____ An act of the will	e. fear the Lord
____ An act of service for another	f. seek the presence of the Lord
____ Silence	g. wait upon the Lord
____ An expression of appreciation	h. intercede

- Think about a worship experience in which one or more of these acts listed below was expressed. Make a note of it in the space provided.

"boast" in God's deeds _____

make high and extol the Lord _____

ascribe greatness to God _____

raise a shout _____

an experience of joy _____

3. *Scripture Study*

- Look up the following Psalms and write out the phrase in each one that speaks to you of worship.

13:5–6 _____

27:14 _____

34:7–10 _____

44:8 _____

46:10 _____

47:1–2 _____

63:1–4 _____

103: 1–5 _____

4. *Application*

- Get ready for the group discussion by thinking about how the words and expressions of praise and worship we have identified relate to the worship of your congregation. Look back over your answers to questions in Sessions 2 and 3 and write below the ways in which the worship of your church does or does not fulfill these injunctions to praise.

- In our worship we fulfill these Old Testament words and expressions of worship in the following ways: _____

_____

_____

_____

_____

_____

◆ In our worship we do not do the following acts of worship, which are described by the words and expressions of Old Testament worship.

_____

_____

_____

_____

_____

_____

PART II: GROUP DISCUSSION

The following questions draw on the study of Part I. Have group members share their insights gained in personal study and learn from each other.

Write on a chalkboard or flip chart all of the group members' answers to the questions in each section.

1. *Life Connection*

◆ Begin each group discussion by having several members of the group share experiences of how they felt when someone remembered and gave thanks for their kindness. Ask several members of the group to tell about their feelings when someone did not remember and give thanks in response to their kindness.

2. *Thought Questions*

◆ How do you use your body in worship?

◆ At what point in worship do you give thanks?

◆ Does the worship in your congregation stretch and inform the mind?

◆ Is the agreement (covenant) God enters into with us made known in worship?

◆ Have you ever experienced the emotion of fear in worship? Describe the experience.

◆ Do you sense that you actually "seek" the presence of the Lord in worship?

- What part does silence play in your worship?
- Is your time of prayer a time for real intercession, or do you think you are just going through the
- motions?
- Does your worship "boast" in God's deeds? Where?
- Does your worship make high and extol the Lord? How?
- Does your worship ascribe greatness for God? Where?
- Do you come away from worship with a feeling of joy?

3. *Scripture Study*

- Read Psalm 150. Describe a worship service in which you felt that the events described in Psalm 150 actually happened. Should this experience of praise be the norm for all worship?
- Read Revelation 5. How many of the characteristics of worship found in the words and expressions of Old Testament worship do you find in this passage? Write them on the chalkboard or flip chart.

4. *Application*

- Spend the last few minutes brainstorming on how the worship of your church could be improved, based on what you have learned in this lesson.

LIFT UP OUR HEARTS

A Study in the New Testament Vocabulary of Worship

In recent years, I have thought often about the concept of being a "model." I've been told to be a "model" husband, a "model" father, a "model" teacher, a "model" Christian, and many models of lesser importance.

I believe in models. They are examples to pattern our lives after and standards that help us in many ways.

In this study, you'll reflect on the concept of "model" and be able to make some connections with your own worship. You will not be studying a model of public worship, such as an order of service, but a more inward model—a model of worship in the heart.

A striking insight into the personal approach to God has been given us by the worship of Jesus. We must not forget that Jesus, whom we worship, is also a worshiper of the Father in the incarnate state. While Jesus was here on earth He gave us a model for worship, a model of praise and adoration that came from the heart (i.e., His regular attendance at the synagogue and temple festivals).

In addition to examining Jesus' model of a worshiper, certain New Testament insights and words will help us wrestle with our own approach to worship. Hopefully, this will help us to improve not only our understanding but also our experience of worship.

WORDS OF THANKSGIVING AND REJOICING

Much of what we are to do in worship is to give thanks and be filled with joy. Unfortunately, many contemporary communities of worship are marked more by boredom and dullness than they are by thanks and joy. Consider these basic understandings of what worship is and study their origins as a way of stimulating your own worship.

- Worship is a continual attitude of thanksgiving.
- Worship is a willingness to rejoice in everything—including the adverse situations of our lives.

SACRED ACCLAMATIONS AND OUTBURSTS OF PRAISE

Worship in our churches today is much more subdued and controlled than it was in biblical times. I can really get into sports events and get excited for my team. I'm not suggesting that we turn the sanctuary into a sports arena, but it does seem strange that we can be so nonchalant about worship. We are celebrating the life, death, and resurrection of Christ and through that the overthrow of the powers of evil. Surely this has to be the most important—and exciting—event in human history. Yet we often go through the motions in a ho-hum and indifferent manner. Perhaps the study of these words of acclamation and praise will help us to break through the barriers of passivity in worship.

- Hallelujah means "Praise Yah!"
- Amen means "You said the truth"
- Maranatha means "Come, our Lord"
- Hosanna! means "0 save!"
- Berahkah means "Blessed"

CHRISTIAN WORSHIP AS CORPORATE

All of us are both personal and public people, and we function a bit differently in each circumstance. For example, I have a personal, intimate relationship with my wife, and I use words and engage in actions at home that would not be appropriate in public. When we are at public gatherings, such as church or social settings, the words and actions I use are appropriate to the setting.

Similarly, we have both a private and a public relationship with the Lord. When I have my personal time of devotion, the words and actions I use are appropriate for the occasion. And then, when 1 gather with the community of faith for worship, the words and actions we use together, while they may have some similarity to private worship, have a slightly different cast, because the setting has changed.

The New Testament words we have studied in this chapter may be used in both personal and corporate worship. The difference is that in corporate worship we say words and do actions together. So we may all give thanks together, or we may all say amen together.

This is what it means to assemble: We come together, as some may say, "to do church." When we worship, we do what the church is called to do.

CONCLUSION

In this study we have faced the need to be responsive in our worship. We want to break through passive worship and become actively engaged. Our Lord left us a model of the attitude of worship we should have. And this attitude, as we have seen, is expressed in a heart full of thanksgiving and joy. When the corporate body comes together to celebrate the death and resurrection of Jesus and His power to overcome sin in our lives, the appropriate corporate response is expressed in words of acclamation and praise. A goal for our private and corporate life is to fulfill this mandate!

STUDY GUIDE

Read Session 6, "Lift Up Our Hearts,"
before starting the study guide.

PART I: PERSONAL STUDY

Complete the following questions individually.

1. *Life Connection*

♦   In this study we want to get into the experience and feeling of the heart. We often use terms to describe what we feel in the heart when we say "My heart is breaking" or "My heart is full of joy." Get in touch with the feelings of your heart by remembering an instance in which you actually felt the emotion of your heart. Write about that experience here:

_____

_____

_____

_____

_____

2. *Content Questions*

♦   Describe in your own words what it means to have an attitude of thanks-giving._____

_____

_____

_____

_____

♦   Describe in your own words what it means to rejoice in everything.

_____

_____

_____

_____

_____

- Match the following acclamations with the most appropriate setting for its expression in worship.

  ___Hallelujah   a. Most appropriate on Palm Sunday

  ___Amen   b. Most appropriate in a Call to Worship

  ___Maranatha   c. Most appropriate in song

  ___Hosanna   d. Most appropriate before Communion

  ___Berehkah (Blessed)   e. Most appropriate at the end of prayer

- What is the difference between private and public worship?

  _____

  _____

  _____

  _____

  _____

3. *Scripture Study*

- In the space provided, write what each of the following New Testament texts says about the heart in worship.

  Rom. 1:21 _____

  Eph. 1:16 _____

  1 Cor. 15:57 _____

  1 Thess. 5:18 _____

  Col. 2:7 _____

  Phil. 4:6 _____

  Heb. 13:15 _____

  Phil. 2:14 _____

  Rom. 5:2–3 _____

  Luke 10:20 _____

  Rev. 19:1, 3–4, 6 _____

  Rom. 1:25 _____

  1 Cor. 16:22 _____

  Eph. 1:3 _____

4. *Application*

Get ready for the group discussion by thinking about the worship of your local church.

Look over the lesson and determine the level of engagement of your heart in worship. How and where in worship do you fulfill these New Testament words of thanksgiving and rejoicing and these sacred acclamations and outbursts of praise? Finish the following sentences.

◆ Worship creates in me a heart of thanksgiving when _____

_____

_____

_____

◆ Worship creates in me a willingness to rejoice when _____

_____

_____

_____

◆ We use the word *hallelujah* in _____

_____

_____

_____

◆ We say the word *amen* after_____

_____

_____

_____

◆ We use the word Maranatha ("Come, our Lord") in _____

_____

_____

_____

◆ We use the word *hosanna* ("0 save") when we _____

_____

_____

_____

◆ The word *blessed* is used when _____

_____

_____

_____

PART II: GROUP DISCUSSION

The following questions draw on the study of Part I. Share the insights you have gained in your personal study and learn from each other.

Write on a chalkboard or flip chart all of the group members' answers to the questions in each section.

1. *Life Connection*

◆ Begin group discussion by asking several members to share a heartfelt experience with the group. Try to get people to describe as deeply as possible the actual feelings they experienced in the heart. This kind of description is hard to do, so don't get discouraged if some people get stuck trying to find adequate words.

2. *Thought Questions*

◆ Does your worship foster a continual attitude of thanksgiving? How?

◆ Does your worship create within you a spirit of rejoicing in everything—even the difficult circumstances of life? How?

◆ Describe the feeling in your heart when you sing "Hallelujah." If a hymn or songbook is handy, look up hymns and songs that use the word *hallelujah*. What are the words and ideas of the verse to which the Hallelujah is sung as a response?

◆ Why should you say "Amen" at the end of prayer?

◆ Why is the word *Maranatha* used in reference to the Lord's Supper?

◆ Why is the word *hosanna* used on Palm Sunday?

◆ Why is the word *blessed* usually used in a call to worship?

3. *Scripture Study*

◆ Read Acts 2:42–47. How many of the words of praise and worship in this lesson can the group find either stated directly or implied in this text? Identify the words in this text that actually refer to the heartfelt response of the people.

◆ Read Revelation 4:9–11. List on the board the words of praise and worship we have discussed in this study that can be found in this text—either directly or implied.

4. *Application*

◆ How do you think the heartfelt response of your own personal worship can be improved?

◆ What do you need to do to achieve a continual attitude of thanksgiving and to rejoice in everything—including the adverse circumstances of life?

TO GOD BE THE GLORY

A Study in the Names of God in Worship

I have always been fascinated by names—particularly the names of people. I wonder: "What is the meaning of this name?" Names given to people, animals, objects, cities, and even streets are laden with history and meaning. This is such a curious and interesting field of inquiry that numerous books have been published to provide people with the meanings of names.

Naming is a powerful activity. All of us who have named children know what a challenge it is to give someone a name.

In biblical thought, the act of naming is striking. Adam, for example, was given the task of naming all the animals. In our time, we associate certain human characteristics with the names of animals. We say someone is "strong as an ox," "quick as a tiger," "smart as a fox," "stubborn as a mule," "gentle as a dove," and so on.

In biblical usage and in worship, God's name is much more than a mere word; it expresses the nature and character of God. To name God or to call upon the name of God is a powerful thing to do and should not be done lightly. To use God's name, even in worship, in a light, joking, or indifferent manner is what it means to take the name of the Lord in vain. On the other hand, to speak the name of God with awe, wonder, and praise is to give glory to God and to honor His name.

Since the name of God is invoked in various ways in our worship—in singing, praying, preaching, testimony, blessings, thanksgiving, benediction, and Communion—it seems highly appropriate to study some of the names of the Father, of the Son, and of the Holy Spirit.

NAMES OF THE FATHER

Here is a summary of many of the names of God the Father and where they may be found in Scripture.

El Shaddai (associated with strength and majesty): Gen. 17:1; 35:11–12
God Most High: Pss. 46:4; 50:14; 91:1; 92:1
Mighty God: Isa. 9:6; 10:21
Eternal God: Isa. 40:28
Living God: Josh. 3:10; 1 Sam. 17:26; Matt. 16:16; 1 Tim. 3:15
Holy One: Isa. 40:25; Hos. 11:9; 2 Kings 19:22; P5. 89:18; Isa. 37:23
Rock: Deut. 32:18; 2 Sam. 22:47; Ps. 18:46; Isa. 8:14; Hab. 1:12

NAMES OF GOD THE SON

We worship not only God the Father, but also God the Son. Here are some of the names of God the Son and where they may be found in Scripture.
Son of God: Matt. 17:5; Mark 1:11; Rom. 1:4
Son of Man: Matt. 8:20; 9:6; Mark 13:26–27
Savior: Luke 2:11; Acts 5:31; 13:23; Phil. 3:20; 2 Tim. 1:10; Titus 2:13
Servant: Matt. 12:18; Acts 3:26; 4:27–30
Word (Logos): John 1:1–2; Heb. 1:1–13; Rev. 19:13
Immanuel (implied as "God with us"): Isa. 7:14; Matt. 28:20
High Priest: Heb. 4:14; 10:21

NAMES OF GOD THE SPIRIT

We also worship God the Spirit. But, while we have many names for God the Father and for God the Son, we have only one name for God the Spirit. While we call God the Spirit the Spirit of God, the Holy Spirit, and the Spirit of Truth, the common designation Spirit. But the word *spirit* is rich with meaning. Here are some of those meanings.

- Holy Spirit distinguishes the Spirit of God as set apart from all other spirits.
- The life force of God is represented by the Spirit of God.
- The Spirit of God "comes upon" or "fills" people to speak and act for God in an anointing.
- God's Spirit is linked with our spirits, particularly in the covenant (2 Cor. 3:5–6).
- The Spirit testifies with our spirits that we are the children of God (Rom. 8:16).
- The Spirit baptizes us into one body (1 Cor. 12:13)
- By the Spirit we confess that Jesus is Lord (1 Cor. 12:3).
- The Spirit prays for us (Rom. 8:26).
- Genuine worship is worship in the Spirit (John 4:24).

Conclusion

This study should help us to remember that all worship is ultimately in the name of God the Father, God the Son, and God the Holy Spirit. We worship the Father through the Son and by the Holy Spirit. And we must not forget that we worship Father, Son, and Holy Spirit.

The Episcopal Church's *Book of Common Prayer* presents a striking expression of worship of the Triune God:

Bishop   Blessed be God: Father, Son, and Holy Spirit.
People   And blessed be his kingdom, now and for ever.

STUDY GUIDE

Read Session 7, "To God Be the Glory,"
before starting the study guide.

PART I: PERSONAL STUDY

Complete the following questions individually.

1. *Life Connection*

* Make some connections with this lesson by reflecting on the meaning of
  names. What is the meaning of your own name? How do you feel when
  someone mispronounces, misspells, or misuses your name? Do the different sounds of your name (said softly, loudly, harshly) provide different responses from you?

2. *Content Questions*

* In this exercise you are to write down the impression you have of each of
  the names listed below. Do not ponder the meaning of these names for a
  long period of rime, but write down what immediately comes to mind.
  El Shaddai _____
  God Most High _____
  Mighty God _____
  Eternal God _____
  Living God _____
  Holy One _____
  Rock _____
  Son of God _____
  Son of Man _____
  Savior _____
  Word _____
  Immanuel_____
  High Priest_____
  Spirit _____

3. *Scripture Study*

◆ Read each Scripture passage listed and write down the name of God revealed in each.

Gen. 17:1 _____

Ps. 18:46 _____

Ps. 50:14 _____

Isa. 9:6 _____

Isa. 40:28 _____

Matt. 9:6 _____

Matt. 12:28 _____

Matt. 28:20 _____

Mark 1:1 _____

Luke 1:32 _____

John 1:1–2 _____

Rom. 8:26 _____

1 Cor. 12:13 _____

1 Tim. 3:15 _____

Heb. 4:14 _____

4. *Application*

(This assignment may take a considerable amount of time. Spend only as much time on it as you have at your disposal.) Get ready for your group discussion by writing beside each name of God a hymn your congregation sings that includes this name.

NAME OF THE SONG   GOD'S NAME

_____   El Shaddai

_____   God Most High

_____   Mighty God

_____   Eternal God

_____   Living God

_____   Holy One

NAME OF THE SONG	GOD'S NAME
_____	Rock
_____	Son of God
_____	Son of Man
_____	Savior
_____	Word
_____	Immanuel
_____	High Priest
_____	Spirit

PART II: GROUP DISCUSSION

The following questions draw on the study of Part I. Share the insights you have gained in your personal study and learn from each other,

Write on a chalkboard or flip chart all of the group members' answers to the questions in each section.

1. *Life Connection*
 - It is important for group members to sense the significance of a name. Ask several persons to share the meaning of their names. Also, ask people to share how they feel when their names are misused.

2. *Thought Questions*
 - Each of us has only one name, but God has many names. What do you think this says about God?
 - What does it mean to take a name in vain? Do you think it is possible to take God's name in vain in worship?
 - One or more of God's names may hold a special meaning for you. State the three most important names of God for you and why they hold such significance for you.
 - If you were to write a song about God's name, which name would you choose? Why? What would you write?

3. *Scripture Study*

♦ Read Revelation 11:15–19. What names of God do you find in this passage? What do these names say about God?

♦ Read Revelation 15:3–4. What names of God do you find in this passage? What do these names say about God?

♦ Read Revelation 19:1–8. What names of God do you find in this passage? What do these names say about God?

4. *Application*

♦ Study the worship of your own church to find how the names of God are used. Look at the hymns and songs, the prayers, Scripture, preaching, the Lord's Supper, and baptism. Do you think the names of God need to be invoked even more? If so, how?

HOLY, HOLY, HOLY!

A Study in the Feeling of Awe in Worship

One of the great tragedies of our Western technological world is the loss of the sense of mystery, awe, and wonder.

I grew up in Africa, where my parents were missionaries. We lived in a clearing in the middle of a jungle area, and I recall how fascinated I was by the jungle with its tall trees, mosses, grasses, bushes, wildflowers, and waterfalls, as well as the birds, monkeys, crocodiles, elephants, lions, and numerous other creatures that inhabited the beautiful, thick greenery of the forest. What attracted me to the forest was its mystery— a mystery I could actually feel. A mystery that provoked awe and wonder within me.

When we returned to the United States, all that mystery seemed to fade away in the presence of a controlled and tamed society of concrete cities. The burgeoning technology of modern civilization seemed to suggest the ultimate intelligence of the human mind over nature. Awe and wonder were to be directed toward the human mind and human powers, rather than to the Creator who makes all things to His glory and praise.

There is an analogy here to worship. Worship should provoke awe and wonder like that of my experience in the forest. But I'm afraid that our Western worship is too much like our technology—controlled, tamed, and rational.

In this study of awe and wonder, I want us to face the need for a greater sense of biblical mystery and awe in our worship!

THE EXPERIENCE OF AWE AND WONDER

We have already seen that words of worship call upon us to acknowledge the surpassing majesty and worth of God. Through words and sacred actions, we ascribe glory to God. And when we see God in all of His glory, the vision of that glory evokes the response of fear and trembling, awe and wonder.

An example of this awe and wonder is presented to us in the experience of Isaiah, who saw God in all of His glory. In response to God's overwhelming otherness, Isaiah saw himself in all of his sinfulness.

I feel this sense of awe when I walk into one of the great ancient cathedrals of the church. Somehow this space speaks to me of the mystery of God's otherness and of God's transcendence and greatness. We need to recapture this sense of awe and mystery today whether we do so through space or through song or through Communion.

As we meditate on the otherness of God, we should nor lose sight of the other truth about God: God is among us and intimate with us. I get this sense from the space of many modern churches and from the way they conduct worship. In many contemporary churches the atmosphere is one of intimacy, friendship, and warmth.

The fact that God is other (transcendent) and intimate (incarnate) is what we call a paradox—a seeming contradiction. It's not a real contradiction but a language that helps us to get at the mystery of God, who is both above us and yet present to us. Ancient worship knew how to express the transcendence of God, and contemporary worship seems to be good at expressing the intimate presence of God. What we need is a worship that expresses both.

MY RESPONSE TO THE OTHERNESS OF GOD

I've always appreciated Isaiah's description of his experience with the living God (see Isa. 6:1–6). It gets at a truth that is really important for all worshipers. And that truth is that we just don't waltz carelessly into the presence of the Holy One. After all, God is God. No matter how good we feel about ourselves or our accomplishments, we are fallen creatures in need of God. So we don't want to walk into worship as though God is lucky we are there. To be in God's presence is to see ourselves for what we are and to throw ourselves at God's mercy and grace. That's what Isaiah did, and God spoke the comforting words to him, assuring Isaiah that he was forgiven and loved. I need to hear those words from God again and again.

AWE RESULTS IN ABANDON

The interesting thing about the experience of God's otherness is that it not only makes us aware of our sinfulness, but also when we hear that we are accepted and loved by the Holy One, there is in us an overwhelming desire to respond to the Holy One in joyful abandonment.

I think this is the reason why I love processions. A procession gives me the sense of coming before the God who accepts me. I've been in both high liturgical settings and low church charismatic settings that have used the procession effectively as a sign-act of coming before the Holy One.

Recently, for example, I visited a mainline seminary where the procession of thirty or so people to an African song of tremendous joy lifted the spirits of the entire congregation to intense expectancy. This procession was only the beginning—a note of joy that remained persistent throughout the service. I think that's what we want to experience in worship; but we need to find ways to do it, and we need to do it with the kind of abandonment that expresses an overwhelming compulsion to respond to the holy.

CONCLUSION

In this study we have attempted to come face to face with the numinous dimension of worship—a sense of awe and wonder, the experience of our own sinfulness, and abandonment to worship the holy. We don't want our worship to be a matter of mere words or rituals. We want it to be an experience of the holy—an experience of the living God!

STUDY GUIDE

*Read Session 8, "Holy, Holy, Holy!,"
before starting the study guide.*

PART I: PERSONAL STUDY

Complete the following questions individually.

1. *Life Connection*

- The best way for us to make a life connection in this lesson is to reflect on and compare two experiences we can recall: (1) an experience of mystery and (2) an experience of learning something in order to understand it better. Record those two experiences below and contrast your feelings about both. _____

   _____

   _____

   _____

2. *Content Questions*

- In worship we acknowledge the_____ of God which provides the response of _____ and _____ .

- What is a paradox? _____

   _____

   _____

   _____

- Name a paradox we experience in worship. _____

   _____

   _____

   _____

- Ancient worship is best at experiencing the _____ of God, while contemporary worship seems best at experiencing the _____ of God.

♦ Why is worship at its best when we experience both the otherness of God and the intimacy of God? _____

_____

_____

_____

♦ What is the implication of the transcendence of God for our worship?

_____

_____

_____

_____

♦ How do you describe awe? _____

_____

_____

_____

♦ What does awe inspire us to experience in worship? _____

_____

_____

_____

3. *Scripture Study*

♦ Write out the characteristic of God's transcendence expressed in each of these verses.

Isa. 6:1-4: _____

_____

_____

Rev. 5:11-13: _____

_____

_____

_____

Ps. 29:9: _____

_____

_____

_____

Ps. 96:11–13: _____

_____

_____

_____

◆ Write out the appropriate response of the worshiper to the transcendence of God as indicated by these verses:

Isa. 6:5: _____

_____

_____

_____

Exod. 3:5:_____

_____

_____

_____

Luke 5:8: _____

_____

_____

_____

4. *Application*

◆ Get ready for the group discussion by thinking about the worship of your church. What do you do in worship that expresses the transcendence of God? What kind of response do you make to the experience of God's otherness?

PART II: GROUP DISCUSSION

The following questions draw on the study of Part I. Share the insights you have gained in your personal study and learn from each other.

Write on a chalkboard or flip chart all of the group members' answers to the questions in each section.

1. *Life Connection*

♦ We can experience God as the other who is high, lifted up, holy, and transcendent. This kind of experience of God is mystery, because words cannot exhaust it or describe it adequately. We can also experience God through God's revelation: the Bible. This kind of experience is more knowable and can be discussed with words of understanding. Start the discussion by asking several people to give an account of experiencing God's mystery in worship.

2. *Thought Questions*

♦ Is the experience of God's mystery an essential aspect of Christian worship? Why?

♦ Would you say that you more often experience understanding or mystery in your worship? Explain.

♦ If you were to choose between an experience of the mystery of God and the understanding of God in your worship, which would you choose? Why?

♦ Do you think biblical worship is primarily mystery or understanding? Why?

3. *Scripture Study*

♦ Examine the following scriptural descriptions of worship for their mystery content. What is going on in each example of worship?

♦ Isa. 6:1–7

♦ Acts 2:42–47

♦ Rev. 4–5

4. *Application*

♦ Examine step by step a typical worship service in your church and decide whether your congregation's worship is (a) mystery dominated or (b) reason dominated. Go back through your service again and determine what you need to do to achieve a balance of mystery and understanding.

PART III

BIBLICAL

INSTITUTIONS

OF

WORSHIP

GOD'S PLACE OF DWELLING

A Study in Tabernacle Worship

 We now turn to the third section of this course: the institutions of worship. To get this third section into focus, let's do a brief review.

In the first section of this study, we observed what God does in worship. In a sentence we can say that God initiates worship just as God initiated a relationship with us. In the Bible we read the story of God's saving deeds toward us, and in worship we tell and act out that story—the story of how God rescues us.

In the second section, we concentrated on how we respond to God's saving action. We respond, of course, in faith, in humility, and in obedience. This response happens in worship, where God's initiative and our response come together. God's initiative is expressed in the story of God's saving deeds, which worship proclaims and enacts. Our response is expressed, as we have seen, in our hearts, in our words, and in the sign-acts we do in worship.

This section now addresses the form, the context, the rituals, and the symbols through which this act of communication between God and God's people takes place.

HOW COMMUNICATION BETWEEN GOD AND GOD'S PEOPLE TAKES PLACE

I communicate with my wife on a regular basis. I stand in front of her and talk to her using the words of everyday life. I communicate to her without words when I put my arms around her and hold her tight. When we go out for dinner, my wife and I talk to each other about issues of the day or the work we are doing. In addition, I sometimes call her on the phone or write a note or send flowers. The point I am trying to make here is that my communication with my wife occurs through such things as words, actions, and symbols and always within some kind of setting.

Worship is an act of communication, A relationship is happening between God and God's people. While this communication is occurring in the heart, there are words, actions, and symbols that are the visible, tangible, concrete means through which this communication is expressed. In other words, we cannot communicate fully without words and actions.

God chooses to communicate with His people in the same way we communicate with each other. In the Old Testament, God chooses to communicate through an institution that uses words and sign-acts—the tabernacle, which we study in this lesson.

WHAT DOES THE PRIEST DO IN THE TABERNACLE?

My work requires me to occasionally make contact with a Christian leader who is very busy and doesn't have the time to answer his own letters or phone calls. Recently, for instance, I needed to ask a Christian leader to support one of my projects with an endorsement. This person is very busy and has an enormous amount of responsibility. Therefore, he is surrounded by a number of people who protect his time by screening phone calls, letters, and other acts of communication by demanding people. In order to get to this person, I had to go through someone whom I knew had access to him. I used a mediator, one who "goes before" and represents one party to another. In the Old Testament tabernacle, a person approached God through such a mediator. Because people could not approach the awesome Holy One of Israel personally, God established a mediator role for the priests, who represented the people before God.

WHAT DOES THE WORSHIPER DO IN THE TABERNACLE?

As I explained above, if I want to get to someone important and speak personally with that person, I must jump through a number of hoops.

Imagine, if you can, how difficult it would be to get to the President of the United States or the head of any other country, for that matter. I don't know the steps for getting to the president, but I know there are many and that a person would have to be quite persistent.

In tabernacle worship, there are some very clear steps that represent the approach to God. These steps are even expressed in the layout of the tabernacle, where one first had to go through the gates and then perform certain actions in the outer court. Only the priests could enter into the inner court, and only the high priest could enter the Holy of Holies, and then only once a year on the Day of Atonement.

THE SIGNIFICANCE OF THE TABERNACLE

Augustine, the great church leader and theologian of the church in the fourth century, said of the signs and symbols of faith, "We see one thing but we apprehend another."

I think this is true of the tabernacle. What we see is an earthly and visible building, a portable one at that. But what we apprehend is something far beyond wood and stone. What we apprehend is:

the conditions for covenant relationship with God;

the presence of God with His people; and

the perfection of God's character.

CONCLUSION

In this study, we have seen that a relationship with God in worship is expressed through tangible signs. In the Old Testament the sign of God's dwelling was the tabernacle. But in the New Testament, God dwells with us in Jesus Christ, who is our high priest and our sacrifice and everything else that is needed to approach God.

So Christian worship is the celebration of the life, the death, the resurrection, and the ever-living priestly ministry of Jesus Christ for us. In worship today we use words and sacred actions—the Bible, water baptism, preaching, and Communion meals—as our visible and tangible signs of a relationship with God through God's Son, Jesus Christ. We need to meditate more deeply on all these words and actions so that we might worship with all our heart.

STUDY GUIDE

Read Session 9, "God's Place of Dwelling,"
before starting the study guide.

PART I: PERSONAL STUDY

Complete the following questions individually.

1. *Life Connection*

◆ Try to remember an incident in which you did not have direct access to a person with whom you wanted to communicate. What procedure did you need to follow to get to this person? How did you feel about the process? Were you angry and frustrated, or did you simply accept the complication of the situation? Write about your experience below.

_____

_____

_____

_____

2. *Content Questions*

◆ In worship, God speaks and acts and we respond. We meet God through words, actions and symbols. Illustrate this with a drawing.

◆ Below is a drawing of the interior space of the tabernacle and a commentary on the steps the worshipers took when making a sacrifice. Read and study this material and answer this question in the space provided: What visible and tangible symbols express the communication going on between God and humanity?

GATES
OUTER COURT
INNER COURT
HOLY OF HOLIES

THE ROLE OF THE WORSHIPER IN
OLD TESTAMENT SACRIFICIAL RITUAL

STEP 1. The person offering the sacrifice must be ceremonially clean. Ritual purity was secured by washing one's clothes and bathing, and in some cases special offerings were presented to the priest (cf. Num. 19:17–21).

STEP 2. The worshiper approached the tabernacle with his or her offering.

STEP 3. The officiating priest received the worshiper, took the sacrificial (animal) victim, and led the worshiper to the altar of burnt offering in the tabernacle courtyard. The family of the worshiper may have watched from the gate or followed the two into the court area to observe from a better vantage point.

STEP 4. After a statement of confession, a prayer, or praise (depending on the type of offering), the worshiper placed his hand on the (animal) victim's head and slit its throat with a knife. (Here the priest would collect the blood to be used in the sacrifice.)

STEP 5. The worshiper, perhaps with the priest's help, would then skin the animal and cut it into quarters. (Once the sacrifice was brought into contact with the layer of burnt offering, the formal priestly duties commenced.)

STEP 6. The worshiper witnessed the priestly activity, including burning the sacrifice on the altar. The worshiper may have responded to the priestly activity in some way, for instance with prayer, silent reflection and meditation, chanting, or singing of liturgical response (depending on the nature of the sacrifice).

STEP 7. After the sacrifice was consumed by fire on the altar, the priest formally dismissed the worshiper with some type of blessing or benediction. In some instances, the worshiper ate a fellowship meal with the priest from the remnant of the sacrificial animal upon completion of the burnt offering. In other cases the remainder of the sacrificial animal was taken home and eaten by the worshiper and his family. The remaining portions of the sacrifice were to be eaten within two days or destroyed by fire (cf. Lev. 19:5–8).

(Andrew Hill, "The Role of the Worshiper in Old Testament Sacrificial Ritual," in *The Biblical Foundations of Christian Worship*, p. 120.)

List all the visible and tangible symbols expressing communications (between God and humans).

3. *Scripture Study*

◆ Read Exodus 25:8. What is the purpose of the tabernacle?

_____

_____

_____

◆ Read Exodus 33:7. What did Moses call the tabernacle?

_____

_____

_____

◆ In Exodus 25–27 there is an elaborate description of the tabernacle, its space and furniture. Scan that material and read Exodus 25:22. What will God do in the tabernacle? _____

_____

_____

_____

◆ Read John 1:14. It is often said that the tabernacle is a foreshadowing of the Incarnation. How so? _____

_____

_____

_____

◆ Read Roman 3:25. It is often said that the tabernacle, as a place of atonement, foreshadowed the atonement made by Jesus Christ. How so?

_____

_____

_____

_____

- Read Hebrew 9:1–10. According to this passage, what is the limitation of the tabernacle? _____
  _____
  _____
  _____
  _____

- Read Hebrew 9:23–28. According to this passage, how does Christ fulfill the symbolism of the tabernacle? _____
  _____
  _____
  _____
  _____

4. *Application*

- The tabernacle was characterized by sacred space, sacred ritual, and a sacred ministry. Evaluate the space, rituals of worship, and functions of the ministry in your worship. How does each facilitate the meeting that takes place between God and the worshiping community? _____
  _____
  _____
  _____
  _____

PART II: GROUP DISCUSSION

The following questions draw on the study of Part I. Share the insights you have gained in your personal study and learn from each other.

Write on a chalkboard or flip chart all of the group members' answers to the questions in each section.

1. *Life Connection*

- Begin your discussion by sharing incidents of not being able to have direct access to some person. After several examples have been given, shift to examples of immediate access to persons. Compare the feeling.

2. Thought Questions

◆ Some people agree that God was approached indirectly in Old Testament times, but directly in New Testament times. What do you think?

◆ Do you think that personal worship in the Old Testament is as direct, as in the Psalms, and that public worship is characterized by a number of words, actions, and symbols that express the point of meeting between God and His people? Comment.

◆ In New Testament times we enjoy a direct relationship to God in personal worship, even as the psalmist did. Do you think it is appropriate to use words, actions, and symbols in Christian public worship as tangible expressions of our approach to God, or do you think we can be without these things in worship?

◆ Some people think the tabernacle provides us with a pattern for Christian worship: (1) We enter the gates, gathering for worship; (2) in the outer court we sing songs, expressing our desire to come to worship; (3) in the inner court we listen to the word of God; and (4) in the Holy of Holies we receive Communion. What do you think? Compare this pattern to the flow of your worship.

3. Scripture Study

◆ Read Exodus 25:8; 25:22; and 33:7. What do you hear these passages saying about what happens in worship?

◆ Read John 1:14 and Roman 3:25. What do these passages say about the place of Jesus Christ in Christian worship?

◆ Read Hebrew 9:1–10, 23–28. Find as many parallels as you can between tabernacle worship and Christian worship. Write these parallels on the board.

4. Application

◆ Evaluate the words, actions, and symbols of your worship. Do you think you "just go through the rituals"? Do you think "we are too careless about our words, actions, and symbols"? On the basis of this study, how do you think you can improve your worship? Would you change the space? Change the order? Change the style? Change the attitudes and hearts of the people? Brainstorm answers to this question.

ENTER HIS COURTS
WITH PRAISE

A Study in Davidic Worship

Because I travel a lot doing workshops on worship in a variety of
different denominations and Christian gatherings, I have the good
fortune of worshiping in nearly every Christian tradition.

One of the conclusions I have come to as a result of experiencing so many
different forms of worship is that there is no one style of worship. However, I'm
convinced there is only one content for Christian worship, and that content is the
story of salvation which culminates in the work of Jesus Christ.

But there are many styles in which this content may be expressed. I love liturgical
worship. I also love to worship with charismatic and all other worshiping communities. Indeed these are very different forms of worship.

I say all this because the worship that we study in this session is so radically
different from the worship of the tabernacle or of the temple.

Tabernacle and temple worship are quite ordered and structured. But Davidic
worship is a lot more free and spontaneous. So here in the Old Testament is one
worship that looks very liturgical and another that looks very free and spontaneous.
God finds both to be pleasing and honoring of His name.

WHAT IS DAVIDIC WORSHIP?

Most of us know about David's worship through the book of Psalms. When I was
a boy, we read a psalm responsively in worship. Today there has been a revival of
psalm singing, and this psalm singing takes us back to Davidic worship. David wrote
many of the Psalms to be sung in worship.

In David's time the tabernacle of Moses was moved to Gibeon, and David set
up a worship center in Zion. This worship center was actually a tent, called David's
Tabernacle.

What's interesting about this tent of meeting and its worship is that it differed substantially from the worship of the tabernacle. In the tent there were no sacrifices. In the tent worship was more free. Worship was led by a team of leaders who conducted worship around the clock. The tent was filled with music, dancers, and people clapping and lifting their hands; they even shouted and had a good time.

THE ORDER OF DAVIDIC WORSHIP

A good way to sense the difference between Davidic worship and the worship of the tabernacle is to look at a possible order of worship. While we don't know the order of Davidic worship exactly, scholar Richard Leonard suggests the possible order below. As you read, go beyond the words and try to picture this worship in your imagination.

The Pilgrimage. Going up to Zion for the festivals was a joyous time for the families of the land. As the worshipers approached the sanctuary, they might have sung the "Psalms of Ascent" (Pss. 120–134), until at last they stood in Jerusalem, "where the tribes go up to praise the name of the LORD" (Ps. 122:4).

The Call to Worship. The trumpet summoned the people for the festival; the lyres and harps of the sanctuary orchestra began to play as the choirs moved into place and took up their song (Ps. 81:1–3).

The Procession. Worshipers had previously gone our on a search for the ark (Pss. 132:6–7), reenactment of the time when it was first brought to Jerusalem. The cry went forth: "Arise, O LORD, and come to your resting place, you and the ark of your might" (Ps. 132:8; cf. Ps. 68:1; Num. 10:35). At this, the appointed Levites begin to carry the ark back to the sanctuary. Their procession was led by dignitaries from the tribes of Israel (Ps. 68:27); it included singers and instrumentalists and young women dancing and playing tambourines (Ps. 68:24–26; 149:3; 150:4).

The Ascent. As the procession mounted the sacred hill, the people acclaimed Yahweh as their "great King," with clapping, the trumpet signal of a king's coronation, and triumphant shouting (Ps. 47:1–5). In joyful psalms, the choir celebrated His dominion over all peoples (Ps. 47:6–9).

The Entrance. As the ark reached the gates of the sacred area, an antiphonal liturgy of entrance occurred, beginning with a hymn of praise (Ps. 24:1–2). The question went forth: "Who may ascend the hill of the

LORD?" The answer came from the priests guarding the entrance: "He who has clean hands and a pure heart." Those in the procession affirmed they met the qualifications (Ps. 24:3–5) and appealed for the doors to be opened so the ark, symbol of the "King of glory," could come in (Ps. 24:7). Dialogue followed, ending with the doorkeeper's question, "Who is this King of glory?" and the answer, "The LORD Almighty [*Yahveh tz'va'ot*] —he is the King of glory" (Ps. 24:8–10).

The Praise of the King. Throughout the festival, the choirs were singing hymns of praise to the Lord similar to those used when the ark had been brought to Zion (Ps. 96; 106; cf. 1 Chron. 16). A favorite may have been the responsive Psalm 136: "Confess to Yahweh, that he is good; for his covenant love is forever" (v. 1, author's translation).

Preparation for the Appearance of the Lord. The festival was to reach its climax at that point when the Lord "appeared" in the midst of his people: "From Zion, perfect in beauty, God shines forth" (Ps. 50:2), perhaps through the liturgical recitation of the covenant commandments (Exod. 20:1–17). In preparation for this high moment, the worship intensified into prophetic song by both choirs and orchestra, occasionally breaking out into the *selah*, or general lifting up of praise, at the announcement of the Lord's coming (Ps. 150:6) or the proclamation of his victories (Ps. 46:8).

One prophetic voice may have come forth, reminding the worshipers of the seriousness with which the Lord regarded their covenant vows and that the disobedient were not to "recite my laws or take my covenant on your lips" (Ps. 50:16).

Renewal of the Covenant. At the proper moment, another prophetic voice was heard, inviting the people to respond with the recitation of the covenant laws: "I am the LORD your God, who brought you up out of Egypt. Open wide your mouth and I will fill it" (Ps. 81:10). Perhaps lifting their hands in oath the congregation reaffirmed with the words they had taught their children (Deut. 6:6–7).

Conclusion. The entire festival was a celebration of the Lord's presence with his people enthroned in their worship and governing their life as a people bound to him.

Aspects of this Davidic worship continued to govern the cult of Judah even after the temple replaced David's simple tent as the home of the ark. Although it is sometimes claimed that the ark remained within the Most Holy Place, which could be entered only once a year by the high priest, this is probably not a correct picture of actual practice. Apparently, the ark was carried out of the sanctuary on occasion until a few decades before the destruction of the temple and the Babylonian Exile. At that time, Josiah ordered the Levites not to carry it anymore (2 Chron. 35:3), an instruction that would have been unnecessary had they not been doing so all along.

(Richard Leonard, "Features of Davidic Worship," *The Biblical Foundations of Christian Worship*, pp. 123–24.)

What Is the Relationship of Davidic Worship to Christian Worship?

I, for one, don't feel at home with tabernacle worship. It's not that I have anything against it; it's that it is all very unfamiliar to me. I'm not used to the sacrificial system and all its rules.

So when I read about Davidic worship I tend to say, "What's this?" It doesn't fit what I know or even expect from the Old Testament. It feels more like New Testament worship.

Some scholars think Davidic worship is a kind of prophetic projection of Christian worship. In Christian worship, sacrifices are not needed because the one final sacrifice for sins has been made in Jesus Christ.

Davidic worship, like Christian worship, calls for the sacrifice of praise and thanksgiving. What God wants from us is not the offering of bulls and goats, but the sacrifice of praise and thanksgiving on our lips and in our lives. God wants the sacrifice of service—lips of humble faith and obedience, a life lived for others.

Conclusion

In this lesson we have seen that there is variety in biblical worship. Even though the established approach to worship was the more formal and precise rituals of the tabernacle, which were prescribed by God, God found David's free and spontaneous worship to be an acceptable act of praise and thanksgiving. What does this mean for our worship today as we seek to worship God with our whole heart?

STUDY GUIDE

Read Session 10, "Enter His Courts with Praise,"
before starting the study guide.

PART I: PERSONAL STUDY

Complete the following questions individually.

1. *Life Connection*

♦ Perhaps you have had the opportunity to worship in both liturgical and
  charismatic settings. If so, describe the similarities and differences of
  those services here. If not, try to remember the most formal or liturgical
  service you have ever experienced and try to remember the most free
  and spontaneous service you have ever attended. Compare them here.

  _____

  _____

  _____

  _____

2. *Content Questions*

♦ Compare the worship of the tabernacle (studied in Session 9) with
  Davidic worship. Write your comparison below. _____

  _____

  _____

  _____

  _____

♦ Prepare an order of the Davidic service in the space provided:

Compare Davidic worship with Christian worship in the columns below:

Davidic Worship	Christian Worship
_____	_____
_____	_____
_____	_____
_____	_____
_____	_____

3. *Scripture Study*

◆ Read Psalm 122. This psalm is one of the "Psalms of Ascent." Outline its progression and content below.

◆ Read Psalm 8 1:1–3. These words may be an ancient call to worship. Below, write what the call tells Israel to do. _____
_____
_____
_____
_____
_____

◆ Read Psalm 68:24–27. This passage describes an ancient worship procession. Draw a picture of the procession or outline the order of the procession in the space below.

- Read Psalm 47. This psalm expresses the praise of the people who have processed to the mountain. List below all the words or phrases of praise in this psalm of ascent. _____

_____

_____

_____

- Read Psalm 24. This is an entrance song, to be sung as the people enter the place of worship. Who may enter and what is the spirit of their praise?

_____

_____

_____

- Read Psalm 136. This psalm may very well have been sung to the praise of the King as the community of worship completed its ascent. Find at least five things for which God is praised. _____

_____

_____

_____

- Read Psalm 46. This psalm may have been a proclamation of the victories of God as He appeared in the assembly of worshipers. What is the appropriate response of the worshiper? See verse 10. _____

_____

_____

_____

- Read Deuteronomy 6:6–7. In the presence of God the community may have reaffirmed its faith. What are the commands they are to keep?

_____

_____

_____

_____

4. *Application*

◆ Get ready for the group discussion by comparing the worship of your church to the description of Davidic worship. What are the similarities and differences?

Similarities: _____

_____

Differences: _____

_____

PART II: GROUP DISCUSSION

The following questions draw on the study of Part I. Share the insights you have gained in your personal study and learn from each other.

Write on a chalkboard or flip chart all of the group members' answers to the questions in each section.

1. *Life Connection*

◆ Begin your discussion by sharing experiences of worship that range from the liturgical to the more free and charismatic forms of worship.

2. *Thought Questions*

◆ What insights does this lesson give you to biblical worship?

◆ Draw lines that represent the progression of Davidic worship.

◆ If you lived in Israel during David's time, would you have preferred tabernacle worship or Davidic worship. Why?

◆ In what ways do you think the worship of David may have foreshadowed the worship in the New Testament?

3. *Scripture Study*

◆ Read Psalm 8 1:1–3. Compare the call to worship in this psalm to the call to worship your congregation uses. What can be learned from this comparison?

- Read Psalm 68:24–2 7. Compare this procession to the style of procession in your congregation. If you do not have one, ask: Should we? What can be learned from this passage?
- Read Psalm 47. Is the worship of this psalm more expressive than your worship? If so, what can be learned about worship from this psalm?
- Read Psalm 136. This psalm praises God for His mighty deeds throughout history. Using the same structure, compose a psalm detailing God's mighty deeds in the community of your church.

4. *Application*
- Compare Davidic worship with the worship of your church, What do you do that Davidic worship does? How does your worship differ? What does Davidic worship do that you do not do? Draw from David's worship to develop an order of worship for your church.

THE HOUSE OF WORSHIP

A Study in Temple Worship

I live in an area in which the construction industry is booming. Everywhere you look new houses are going up—almost overnight, it seems. One thing my wife and I like to do is to go to the open house showings of these new homes. We live an old Victorian house with very small closets and one small bathroom, so we enjoy oohing and ahhing over the large walk-in closets and the huge bathrooms with double sinks in these houses.

But more important, we like to imagine what it would be like to live there—how we would furnish and decorate it. But then we go home, walk into our old house, and enthusiastically say, "You can't replace the charm of an older home. Look at our woodwork, the high ceilings, and the quaint aspects of this old Victorian. This is us. This is our place, the place where we belong."

Place is very important. All of us want a place that we call our own. When we think about place and how important it is to us, we can make some connections with this session, which emphasizes the place of worship. You see, God said, "Have them make a sanctuary for me, and I will dwell among them" (Exod. 25:8).

WHY A PLACE FOR GOD?

At first it seems contradictory that God would want a place, a house for Himself in the midst of Israel, His people. Why does God need a dwelling place? Isn't His place in the heavens? Doesn't He dwell in a place not made of stone or with human hands? What need does God have of a temple?

Remember that Israel was set in the middle of pagan nations and peoples—peoples who had temples and rituals that represented their gods. The reason why God wanted a home, a house of worship among His people, was that God wanted a place where God and His acts among the people would be remembered.

What is interesting to me about this desire of God's is that it is exactly what we do at worship. We remember God's acts of mercy and salvation through the word and sacred actions that proclaim and enact God's acts of salvation. And we generally do this in a particular place—the church building, the house where God's people gather.

But Israel often got too invested in the form through which God's acts of salvation were presented. This is what Stephen chided Israel for in New Testament times, thus echoing the message of the prophets (Acts 7:47–49). Today, we face the same problem. We become too invested in the house of worship (the building) and in its furniture (the form of worship) and forget the One who dwells there and whose actions for our salvation have become lost behind the form in which we have become so invested. Of course, there is nothing wrong with form itself; it is form for the sake of form that we need to avoid.

SACRED SYMBOLS, SACRED RITUALS, SACRED MINISTRY

I like form. I am persuaded that God has no problem with form. After all, God created form, and God became form through the Incarnation. The world sees and knows God in the form of a man—Jesus Christ.

Jesus was no ghost. He was a real man—a man of flesh and blood, hair and fingernails, body and soul, spirit and matter. The Incarnation affirms the principle that the Divine encounters us through the human, or to put it another way, the immaterial communicates through the material.

This principle of the Incarnation is foreshadowed in the temple. In the temple, God resided with and met with His people through tangible symbols, sacred rituals, and a sacred mystery.

Through these visible, tangible, concrete signs, the families of Israel came to worship God.

FAMILY WORSHIP IN THE TEMPLE

I believe in individual worship. That is, I believe it is important for each person to set aside a time to be alone with God.

I also believe in corporate worship. It is imperative for us to come together with other believers in a time of public praise and worship.

I also believe in family worship. Mothers and dads and children need to have time together to worship God.

All three of these approaches to worship are found in the Old Testament. But here are some special occasions for family worship:

* On the eighth day of a child's life he was brought for circumcision (Lev. 12:3; cf. Luke 2:22–24).
* Firstborn animals were presented as a family sacrifice at particular seasons (Exod. 22:30).
* A basket of first fruit was offered at the beginning of harvest season (Exod. 23:19).
* At the end of harvest, a tenth was presented to the Lord (Num. 18:21–32).
* Sacrifices could be offered for personal reasons (Gen. 28:18–22).
* Serious sin or sickness were reasons for sacrifice (Lev. 4–6; 13:15).

FESTIVALS IN THE TEMPLE

I love a good feast! As a matter of fact, I think most people do. One of the striking features of Old Testament worship is the feast.

In the feasts Israel did what worship does. They remembered, and they celebrated. It is a simple fact that most churches have lost what is absolutely central to Christian worship: remembering in the context of feast.

Christian feasts are all rooted in the Christian year (Advent, Christmas, Epiphany, Lent, Holy Week, Easter, Pentecost), each season of which celebrates a different facet of God's saving work.

FEAST	WORK OF CHRIST
Advent	We wait for the coming of Christ.
Christmas	Christ is born.
Epiphany	We manifest and proclaim Christ to the world.
Lent	We prepare for Jesus' death.
Holy Week	We enter the death.
Easter	We celebrate our resurrection with the Lord.
Pentecost	We celebrate the coming of the Holy Spirit in our lives.

I mention these feasts because I think they are either forgotten or are practiced in a perfunctory way in most churches.

The same was true of Israel. The people of Israel had all these wonderful feasts. In some periods of time they forgot to celebrate them; at other times they celebrated them, but lost their meaning. Here is a list of the four major feasts:

Passover (April)   Feast of Booths (October)
Feast of Weeks (May)   Day of Atonement

CONCLUSION

In this session we have seen that God commanded that a house of worship be established where He could dwell with the people. We learn from this that there is nothing wrong with a place of worship.

In New Testament times we confess that God lives in us, and when we come together in a place that houses the worshiper, God is among us.

So this session raises some questions for us: What is the role of the building? What should we do in the building to celebrate God's great acts of salvation? What should the family do? How should we celebrate God's saving deeds? As we face these questions, we learn more and more about worshiping God with our whole heart.

STUDY GUIDE

Read Session 11, "The House of Worship,"
before starting the study guide.

PART I: PERSONAL STORY

Complete the following questions individually.

1. *Life Connection*

◆ Begin thinking about the house of worship by asking yourself one simple question: "How does the house that I live in reflect me?" You may want to think of arrangement of space, furnishings, and the things you do in that house as a place of your dwelling. Is it stuffy, formal, casual, etc.? Would someone say, "Oh, this house looks just like you"? Write your reflections here: _____

_____

_____

_____

_____

2. *Content Questions*

◆ Why does God want a home, a place of dwelling among His people?

_____

_____

_____

_____

◆ How did the house in which God dwelt become a problem for Israel?

_____

_____

_____

_____

_____

◆ Do you think we sometimes become too invested in the house of God and forget to worship the God who dwells there? Give an example.

_____

_____

_____

_____

◆ What is the principle of the Incarnation? _____

_____

_____

_____

◆ What does the principle of the Incarnation say about tangible symbols, sacred rituals, and sacred mystery? _____

_____

_____

_____

◆ In your own words, name at least two reasons why families worshiped in the temple._____

_____

_____

_____

◆ Name at least one feast celebrated in the temple. _____

_____

_____

_____

3. *Scripture Study*
◆ Read 1 Kings 8:27–30. What do you think is the most important matter this passage states regarding the temple? _____

_____

_____

- Read Acts 7:48–49. Why do you think Stephen's statement made the Jews angry enough to stone him to death? _____

  _____

  _____

  _____

  _____

- Read 2 Chronicles 6:7–11. Why was the temple built? _____

  _____

  _____

  _____

  _____

- Read John 2:19–21. What does it mean for Jesus to compare Himself to the temple? _____

  _____

  _____

  _____

  _____

- Read Psalms 68:24–27. Here is a description of a festival procession. Describe the procession in your own words _____

  _____

  _____

  _____

  _____

4. *Application*

- Begin to prepare for the group discussion by thinking about the relationship the temple sustains to New Testament worship. Write down as many parallels as come to mind from the study of this lesson.

PART II: GROUP DISCUSSION

The following questions draw on the study of Part I. Share the insights you have gained in your personal study and learn from each other.

Write on a chalkboard or flip chart all of the group members' answers to the questions in each section.

1. *Life Connection*

+ Begin by asking several people to discuss how their homes are reflections of themselves. Ask several persons to share how they think a friend's home (another person in the class) reflects the personality and ambiance of its owner.

2. *Thought Questions*

+ Do you think God wants the house of worship to reflect the God who dwells there?

+ Does the Old Testament practice of using signs and symbols to represent the presence of God pertain to modern church buildings as well? Why?

+ Do you think Christian houses of worship should be plain or private? Why?

+ Comment on the feeling of worship you experience in a plain church building and the feeling you experience in a cathedral or other church building that is considered a work of art.

+ What specific family services should occur in the Christian church building?

+ What kinds of feasts and festivals should be celebrated in the church building?

+ What does it mean to know that you are the temple of God, that God dwells within you?

3. *Scripture Study*

+ Compare 1 Kings 8:37–40 and Acts 7:48–49. How do you understand the message of these verses?

+ Read 2 Chronicles 6:7–11. Do you think God wanted the temple to be built? Do you think God allowed the building of the temple as an accommodation to our need to have tangible symbols? If the latter, do you think it is wrong to desire tangible symbols? Do you think we sometimes worship the house of God more than the God who dwells there? If so, how? Do you think we sometimes pay too little attention to the house of worship? If so, how? And what should we do about it?

- Read 1 Corinthians 3:16–17. What does it mean to know that "you are that temple"? How should this truth change your behavior?

4. *Application*

- Evaluate the place in which you worship and ask yourself these questions:
- Does God feel welcome here?
- What tangible signs of God's presence are expressed in our house of worship?
- Should we remove all Christian symbolism from our house of worship?
- Should we include more symbols of God's presence in our house of worship?
- Does God dwell in the hearts of our people?

ASSEMBLE THE PEOPLE

A Study in Synagogue Worship

In my home I was always taught to have a profound respect and love for God's people, the Jews. My dad loved the Old Testament and often preached from it. He also loved the Jewish people and frequently emulated their traditions of piety.

One of the traditions he practiced was care for the Bible as a sacred book. He not only read the Bible on a regular basis, but he actually wore out his own personal Bible on more than one occasion as well.

I remember one incident as though it was yesterday. I was walking through the dining room of our parsonage and noticed my dad in the kitchen, wrapping his Bible in newspaper.

Naturally, I was curious about what he was doing. I asked in a tone of great surprise, "Dad, what are you doing?"

He calmly replied, "Well, I love my worn-out Bible, so I'm going to bury it. Right now I'm preparing the Bible for burial. You don't just throw old Bibles into the trash, you know—it's the Word of God. You have to treat it with reverence."

I went with my dad into the backyard and watched as he prayerfully laid his old and worn-out Bible to rest in the ground. That action delivered a message to me that I've never forgotten. As a matter of fact, I once told this story to a rabbi, who exclaimed with great joy, "Your father is a Jew!"

I tell you this story because it's important for all of us who desire to worship God with all our hearts to know that the Jewish worship tradition, especially the worship of the synagogue, was a powerful influence on early Christian worship.

SYNAGOGUE WORSHIP

We don't have any actual services from the first-century synagogue worship, but we do have a good knowledge of the content of worship. It was ordered around praise, prayer, and instruction.

PRAISE

Hebrew worship began with praise. This was in accord with the principle laid down in the Talmud: "Man should always utter praises, and then pray." It is very possible that Christian worship also began with praise. First Corinthians 14:26 suggests that at the head of the list of corporate worship "a hymn" should be sung.

We also know that the ruler of the synagogue invited someone to commence worship with a call to worship (Luke 4:20). The leader began with the cry "Bless ye the Lord, the One who is to be blessed," and the people responded, "Blessed be the Lord forever."

PRAYER

We do not have any of the actual first-century prayers, but we do know that they consisted of a number of sections and that each one ended with a blessing. By the end of the first century these prayers were standardized so that there were seven on the Sabbath and eighteen in the daily worship. These prayers are called *Tefillah*, which is a Hebrew word meaning "prayer."

It is possible that we can gain a sense of these ancient prayers through the study of the later, more developed Eighteen Benedictions.

INSTRUCTION

One thing we know for certain about first-century synagogue worship is that worshipers read a considerable amount of Scripture (see Luke 4:16–27; Acts 13:15, 27; 15:21). Portions of the Pentateuch and the Prophets were read on a regular basis. The practice of commenting on and explaining these passages was a normal part of worship. Any male member of the congregation could be invited to read from the Law and the Prophets and to expound on the reading (Luke 4:16–27).

Christian worship today is still very much like synagogue worship. We offer praise to God, especially through song, and we tell the story of salvation, especially through the reading and expounding of Scripture. In addition, the church met in houses for the agape feast, which became our Lord's Supper, or Eucharist (more about this in the next session).

SYNAGOGUE SPACE

I've already expressed my interest in space, and the space of the synagogue is no exception in terms of interest and meaning.

Basically, the synagogue was arranged in such a way that its space spoke of the central conviction of Jewish faith. Here is a summary:

- The focus of the synagogue was the ark (here God was enthroned invisibly).
- In front of the ark was the veil and the seven-branched candle stand (connection with the tabernacle).
- Another focus of the synagogue was the bema (here the Scriptures were read and expounded upon).
- All synagogues faced Jerusalem (in expectation of the promised land).

Conclusion

Now we must ask: How does the worship of the synagogue shape our Christian experience? Can we, like the early Christians, learn something from our Jewish roots that will help us worship God with all our hearts? If so, what and how?

STUDY GUIDE

Read Session 12, "Assemble the People,"
before starting the study guide.

PART I: PERSONAL STUDY

Complete the following questions individually.

1. *Life Connection*

◆ Many Christians have had the experience of attending a synagogue or, at least of passing through a synagogue. If you have had this experience, write your memories of it below. If not, try to find some time soon to attend a synagogue service or to at least visit a synagogue. Jews are very welcoming people and will be happy to have you visit with them,

2. *Content Questions*

◆ What is the principle of praise laid down in the Talmud? _____

_____

_____

_____

_____

◆ Write a Jewish call to worship below. _____

_____

_____

_____

_____

◆ What is the Hebrew Word for "prayer"?_____

_____

_____

_____

_____

◆ What role did the Word of God play in Jewish worship? _____

_____

_____

_____

_____

♦ Below is a graph of synagogue space. Fill in the function of the various parts of its space.

Jerusalem   Function

Ark
Lectern
Seats

♦ What impact did the synagogue have on Christian worship? _____

_____

_____

_____

_____

3. *Scripture Study*

♦ Read 1 Corinthians 14:26. Do you think this comment may reflect the Talmud teaching "Man should always offer praises, and then pray"?

_____

_____

_____

_____

♦ Read Luke 4:16–30. What does this passage tell us about synagogue worship in the first century? List all the features you can find. _____

_____

_____

_____

_____

◆ Read Acts 13:13–43. What do verses 15 and 27 say about the use of Scripture in synagogue worship? _____

_____

_____

_____

◆ Read Acts 15:21. How was Scripture used in synagogue worship?

_____

_____

_____

_____

_____

4. *Application*

◆ Although the insights into synagogue worship of the first century are somewhat sparse, some insight into synagogue worship and the impact it made on Christian worship can be gained by a study of the above passages. Write here what Christian worship has in common with synagogue worship. _____

_____

_____

_____

_____

PART II: GROUP DISCUSSION

The following questions draw on the study of Part I. Share the insights you have gained in your personal study and learn from each other.

Write on a chalkboard or flip chart all of the group members' answers to the questions in each section.

1. *Life Connection*

◆ Begin your discussion by asking those who have been to a synagogue worship or who have visited a synagogue to talk about their experience.

2. Thought Questions

+ Ask each person in the group to comment on the Talmud prescription "Man should always utter praises, then pray."

+ Should Christian worship follow this prescription and begin with praise?

+ If you answered yes to the above question, ask each person to suggest a praise hymn, song, or Scripture passage that he or she would like to use as the opening praise of worship. (Do this in the spirit of 1 Cor. 14:26.)

+ Study each of the words in the call to worship: "Bless ye the Lord, the one who is to be blessed; Blessed be the Lord forever." What is the spirit of this call to worship?

+ What kind of a call to worship do you think the Christian church should use? Can you find one or more in Scripture?

+ Do you think Christian churches should follow the Jewish custom of ascribing spiritual value to its space and the placement of its worship furniture (like the pulpit, the Table, and the baptismal pool or font)?

3. Scripture Study

+ Read 1 Corinthians 14:26. Should we all come to worship with a song or hymn or some other act of praise? This is called "open worship" and is a form of worship urged by some today.

+ Read Luke 16:30. Share insights from the personal study. What does this passage reveal about synagogue worship in the first century? List everyone's answers.

+ Read Psalms 103:1–5. How would you create a call to worship from this passage? Take time to do it and put it on the board.

+ Read Acts 2:42–47. What do you find in this description of worship, which may have come from the synagogue? What are some new elements that are distinctly Christian elements of worship?

4. Application

+ Using insights from this lesson, create an order of worship that reflects the impact of synagogue worship in the church.

O COME, LET US WORSHIP

A Study in New Testament Worship

 Language has always been an important part of my life. I make living by speaking and writing, so naturally I am greatly indebted to language.

But in recent years I have learned that there is more to language than words. The more I teach and write, and the more I read and study the Scripture and church history, the more I am aware of how pictures are a kind of language.

For example, when I read a book and think about its contents, I always try to capture the idea that I'm reading about in some kind of graph or picture language.

Sometimes when a person is explaining something to me, I'll ask, "Can you draw me picture of that or can you put it in words that will make that idea clearer to me?"

Interestingly, the Bible frequently speaks to us through picture words. Both the church and its worship can be pictured.

In this lesson we will concentrate on the picture communication of New Testament worship. Let's begin by understanding the pictures of the church.

NEW TESTAMENT PICTURES OF THE CHURCH

I remember the time somebody asked me to define *church*. I was stumped. There is no such thing as a propositional definition of the church.

The more I thought about the question, the more I realized that the church is not as easily defined as it is pictured. Here are some of the major pictures of the church in the New Testament:

- The church is a *body* (1 Cor. 12:13; Eph. 4:4).
- The church is a *flock* protected by its *shepherd* (Acts 20:28; 1 Pet. 5:2–3).
- The church is *branches* nourished by the *vine* (John 15:1–6) or
- The *olive tree* (Rom. 11:16–21).

- The church is compared to a *city*, particularly *Jerusalem* (Gal. 4:26; Heb. 12:22; 13:14; Rev. 21:2).
- The church is a *household* of faith (Gal. 6:10; Eph. 2:19).
- The church is the *bride* of Christ (Rev. 19:7; 21:2).
- The church is the *temple* of the Holy Spirit (1 Cor. 3:16–17; 2 Cor. 6:16).
- The church is a *new creation* (2 Cor. 5:17).

Here in all of this picture language is an attempt to grasp the reality of the church, which cannot be conveyed in a technical, rational language. What, do we ask, do these picture words mean for our worship?

PICTURES OF WORSHIP IN THE EARLY CHURCH

In the early church there probably was an unusual amount of enthusiasm and intimacy. I don't know if you have ever participated in a new church or not, but my experience is that people in new churches, before they become institutionalized, enjoy being together and fellowship with a considerable amount of enthusiasm.

If we want to worship God with all of our hearts, we need to keep this first love experience.

Today we are asking "What did they do in the early church that was so exciting?"

We know *what* they did in early church worship, and we can emulate that. But there is no magic by which we can recover the *spirit* in which the early Christians worshiped. The best we can do is to bring faith, intention, and participation into our worship. In no way can we dismiss the importance of this fact.

Here, then, are some picture words of the worship of the early church:

- They met in private homes (Acts 2:46),
- They met on the first day of the week (Acts 20:7; 1 Cor. 16:20).
- They sang hymns (Eph. 5:19).
- They prayed together (1 Cor. 11:4–5).
- They heard instruction (1 Cor. 14:26; Col. 3:16).
- They focused on the Lord's Supper (1 Cor. 10:16–17; 11:20–29; Acts 2:42).
- They sang in tongues with interpretation and prophecy (1 Cor. 11:4–5; 14:1–33).
- Prophets seemed to have a role in corporate worship (1 Cor. 14:23–33).
- Worship happened in the context of good fellowship (Acts 2:42).
- Worship inspired compassion toward the poor (Acts 2:44–45).
- Worshipers were filled with awe and joy (Acts 2:43).

Unfortunately, we do not know a great deal about the order of worship in the New Testament. Acts 2:42 suggests that worship consisted of two primary actions: the preaching, reaching, and storytelling of the apostles and the celebration of the presence of the resurrected Christ at the breaking of the bread. (As Jesus was known in the breaking of the bread on the road to Emmaus and in the upper room, so they experienced the mystery of the resurrected Christ as the regular worship event of breaking bread; Luke 24:28–31, 35.)

From the insights of the Corinthian correspondence (particularly 1 Cor. 11, 12, 14) we see a picture of a considerable amount of free worship, of the preaching of the Word, and of the celebration of the Table. Also, Revelation 4 and 5 provide us a picture of the vision of a more liturgical worship.

A thorough investigation of these pictures is beyond the scope of this study. The study of the history of Christian worship gives us more insight into the *how* of worship, whereas the *what* of worship is grounded in the Scripture.

CONCLUSION

This study has presented us with the pictures of New Testament worship. While the Scripture presents snapshots of the action of worship, we don't have a vision of a whole service. But we do know this: The New Testament clearly pictures the *what* of worship— preaching, breaking bread, singing, and praying in the context of fellowship are at the heart of worship. We study the history of worship to find out *how* Christians have put all these *whats* of worship into practice from century to century. To investigate the *how* of worship, study the material of the second course in this series, *Discovering the Missing Jewel: A Study in Worship Through the Centuries*. In the meantime, continue to worship with all your heart!

STUDY GUIDE

Read Session 13, "O Come, Let Us Worship,"
before starting the study guide.

PART I: PERSONAL STUDY

Complete the following questions individually.

1. *Life Connection*

♦ Think about the most moving worship service you have ever attended.
  What was so significant about this worship? Recall as much as you can
  and write it below. _____

  _____

  _____

  _____

  _____

2. *Content Questions*

♦ The text of this lesson lists eight picture words of the church in the New
  Testament. Choose three of these picture words and draw them below,
  Under each picture word, write a phrase that summarizes why this pic-
  ture word is important for you.

♦ The text of this lesson provides eleven picture words for worship. In the
  space below, draw at least three of these picture words and write a
  phrase that expresses the importance of this picture.

+ The text of this lesson describes three kinds of worship-house church worship (Acts 2:42–47), body worship (1 Cor. 14), and liturgical worship (Rev. 4–5). Draw a picture of one of these styles of worship.

3. *Scripture Study*
+ Read Acts 2:42–47 (house church worship). List all the elements of worship below: _____
_____
_____
_____
_____

+ Read 1 Corinthians 14. List all the elements of free worship below:
_____
_____
_____
_____

+ Read Revelation 4–5. List all the elements of liturgical worship below:
_____
_____
_____
_____

+ Read 1 Corinthians 11:23–26. In what way is this worship action distinctly different from anything in the synagogue? What is the significance of the Lord's Supper?

_____
_____
_____
_____

4. *Application*

◆ Get ready for the group discussion by thinking about the importance of these New Testament pictures for the worship of your church. Which picture best describes your worship style? What can you learn from the other pictures? _____

_____

_____

_____

_____

PART II: GROUP DISCUSSION

The following questions draw on the study of Part I. Share the insights you have gained in your personal study and learn from each other.

Write on a chalkboard or flip chart all of the group members' answers to the questions in each section.

1. *Life Connection*

◆ Begin your discussion by asking several people to present their most memorable worship experience.

◆ Write on a chalkboard or flip chart all of the group members' answers to the questions in each section.

2. *Thought Questions*

◆ Does it surprise you that there are different pictures of worship styles in the New Testament?

◆ How would you respond to someone who says that God expects us to all use the same style of worship?

◆ What is the style of worship in your own church?

◆ What is the special contribution of each style of worship?

◆ Which of these styles of worship is the most comfortable for you? Why?

- Which of these styles of worship is the least comfortable to you? Why?
- What perceptions do you have about the worship style that is most threatening to you? Why?
- How would you respond if you were told that the future of worship was the convergence of the various styles?

3. *Scripture Study*

- Read Acts 2:42–47. What do you find in this style of worship that (a) you like, (b) threatens you?
- Read 1 Corinthians 12. What do you find in this style of worship that (a) you like, (b) threatens you?
- Read Revelation 4–5. What do you find in this style of worship that (a) you like, (b) threatens you?
- Read 1 Corinthians 11:23–26. How frequently do you think the church should celebrate the Table of the Lord? Why?

4. *Application*

- Since this is the last class of *Learning How to Worship with All Your Heart*, do a summary of the whole course. Ask: What did you learn from this course that helps you understand worship better? Ask: Should we make any changes in our worship on the basis of what we have learned?